Rebuild

Rebuild

Small groups can make a difference

edited by Fran Beckett

Fran Beckett
Brendan Bowles
Julia Burton-Jones
Steve Chalke
Sharon Craddock
Roy Crowne
Paul Dicken
Joel Edwards
Jill Garner
Andy Hawthorne
Eileen Jones
Nina Kelly
David Partington
Simon Pellew
Mannie Stewart
Sarah Thomas
Keith Tondeur
Rob Warner
Keith White

Crossway Books

Leicester

CROSSWAY BOOKS
38 De Montfort Street, Leicester LE1 7GP, England

First published 2001

British Library Cataloguing in Publication Data
A catalogue record for this book is available from the British Library.

ISBN 1–85684–205–3

Set in Palatino
Typeset in Great Britain
Printed in Great Britain

CONTENTS

Why this book?
Steve Chalke   7

The EDEN Project: bringing hope
Andy Hawthorne   11

A health warning for leaders   13

Part One: Preparing for action

1   God's passion for people
    Fran Beckett   19

2   Salt and light
    Fran Beckett   24

3   Listeners first
    Fran Beckett   30

4   Finding a focus
    Fran Beckett   37

5   Where angels fear to tread: preparing for action
    Jill Garner   45

Part Two: Into the community

6   Neighbourhood impact
    Mannie Stewart   57

7   Supporting families under pressure
    Nina Kelly and Eileen Jones   65

8   Money worries
    Keith Tondeur   73

9   Caring for the carers
    Julia Burton-Jones   80

10 Support for older people
    Sharon Craddock   89

11 People with disabilities
    Paul Dicken   98

12 Literacy and work
    Simon Pellew and Sarah Thomas   107

13 Homelessness
    Brendan Bowles   115

14 Children with a future
    Keith White   124

15 Twenty-first century youth
    Roy Crowne   133

16 Tackling addiction
    David Partington   141

17 Prison: during and after
    Peter Zimmerman   150

    What place the gospel? Social action
    and evangelism
    Rob Warner   157

    The last word
    Joel Edwards   165

    List of contributors   167

Why this book?

Steve Chalke

The term 'synagogue' never appears in the Old Testament. Why not? The answer is simple – there weren't any synagogues in Old Testament Israel. I didn't realize this until I sat one evening with my concordance trying to find a reference to 'synagogue'. I guess you're now thinking, 'Get a life, Steve!' But that sad evening on my own led me to change my whole view of the role church plays in our society. You see, if the Israelites didn't have synagogues to worship in, where did they go? I find most people quickly answer, 'The temple.' But the reality is somewhat different.

Though the temple was used by the people for worship this would only be for special occasions a few times a year. The main week-by-week, day-by-day worship would have taken place at home with the family. Now, before you think that 2.4 children in the Jewish equivalent of a suburban-semi house church doesn't sound that exciting, remember that in Hebrew society the family was an extended one, far from the nuclear type we are used to. All kinds of relatives and friends would have gathered together. The home was a rich, inclusive environment, a place not only for worship or entertainment, but also for physical and emotional sustenance, somewhere to be nursed when sick, or to take away loneliness, and a home when retirement came.

When we use the term 'extended' we make a big mistake. We presuppose that the nuclear family is normal. But an African tribal leader once told me that in Africa they do not have the 'extended' family; they have the 'normal' family. 'And,' he added, 'your Western experiment with the "nuclear" family, or what should really be called the "shrunken" family, has failed because it is unable to sustain community.'

When we can't sustain an inclusive community we both

impoverish ourselves and sadden God. That's why in the Old Testament we hear him again and again remind the Hebrew people to remember the orphan, the widow and the refugee. Why? Because they were the three categories of people who could fall outside the arms of community, the extended family. God shouts to his people, 'Get them back in!'

Synagogues finally arrived during the intertestamental period – those 400 years between the Old and New Testaments. They developed as a secondary structure to support the extended family in maintaining the community. And it was out of the synagogues that the first Christian churches raised their heads. In fact, though it is often claimed that Peter, James and the other apostles set about a programme of church planting, more accurately what they engaged in was the establishment of a series of messianic synagogues. It took Paul finally to strip synagogues of their Jewish clothing and think about what church for gentiles should look like – though even for him community was the foundation of his understanding.

So if we were to ask Jesus how he would engage his local synagogue with the community he would look at us in disbelief: for him the two were inseparable. Twenty centuries later this important book challenges us to consider how to recapture the church's role at the heart of our communities – to question how we rebuild, not just our links *with* the community, but return our churches to *being* the hub of the community.

Jesus was often asked, 'What will the Kingdom of God be like?' For that question he had many answers (and the church down the years has had a few of its own). One way Jesus answered the question was to tell the Parable of the Talents. Now, parables are not always the easiest of stories to understand and this one is no exception. Most of us at some stage have probably heard a sermon on this parable, studied it at a house group, or even wrestled with it on our own. More often than not the thing that distracts us is the word 'talents' – leading us to try to work out how our talent for balancing a spoon on the end of our nose can be put to use for God so that we don't get left outside where all that crying and teeth grinding goes on. But that's not the point of the parable at all.

I like to think of the servant who was given five talents in this way. He takes what the master has given him and invests them. The investment fails and he loses two. But he learns some valuable lessons from his mistakes, uses the remaining three in a better deal and ends up with seven. He then risks these seven and increases his talents to fifteen. Unfortunately just before the master returns there is a downturn in the market and he loses five. The master, however, looks favourably on him because he didn't simply bury what he was given but risked it, and in risking made a profit.

Often we treat what we have in our churches as so precious that we end up acting like the wicked, lazy servant who buries his talent in the ground in order to keep it safe. We see our task as faithfully protecting and passing on that which was delivered to us – intact and unchanged. The point of Jesus' parable, however, is to inspire us do the opposite. Jesus is saying that the treasure of the gospel is never honoured when buried in the ground for 'safe-keeping'. Instead he entrusts it to us to be risked.

Archbishop Robert Runcie pointed out that the church will never learn from its mistakes until it is prepared to make some. Jesus is looking for followers who are *risk takers* and *mistake makers*. As this book informs and inspires you it will also ask you to take risks but, as the parable of the talents suggests, risks deliver rewards!

The EDEN Project: bringing hope

Andy Hawthorne

John, as one of twelve children, had a childhood of neglect and abuse. He lived in one institution after another, and then was homeless, out on the streets. The two Christians who invited him to hear the gospel gave him far more than an encouraging hug when he committed his life to Jesus. They took him into their home and shared their lives with him for several years, helping him to work through his numerous problems.

Jesus showed us that sharing the gospel means caring for the whole person, whether it is buying people a cup of tea, taking time to be a friend, praying for them, or even taking them into your home.

In Manchester we have been on a steep learning-curve, discovering exactly what it means to reach out to the young people of our city. Many, through the schools work of The World Wide Message Tribe, were responding to the good news that Jesus offers. But we were tired of seeing them fall away, rather than growing up into lifelong disciples. Most were in difficult situations and had family problems, and there were few churches who were willing and able to take these young people on and work with them in a way young people could relate to.

While we were thinking and praying about this God challenged us to do something about it. This is why EDEN was born. EDEN is about urban regeneration, not of buildings or housing estates, but of people and com-munities. It's about making a long-term, significant impact on some of the toughest areas of the city by getting involved in the community at every level. It's about helping our neighbours, being there for people we wouldn't normally mix with, getting involved in local schools. It's about working alongside existing social action initiatives or starting new ones if necessary. It's about being committed to the local church, not just for our own benefit, but also to see young people being given every opportunity to hear the message of Jesus in a way that makes sense, and to get to know him for themselves. It's about not giving up when people throw stones at our house, steal our car, shout abuse in the street or write us off as naïve. It's about our whole life.

The way EDEN works is for about thirty volunteer youth workers to move into an area like Wythenshawe or Salford, with a full-time team of three or four, all linked to a local church. The team works largely in schools through assemblies, lessons, lunchtime clubs and after-school activities to build relationships and reach as many young people as possible. The volunteers have full-time jobs but work with EDEN in the evenings and at weekends helping with youth clubs, social projects, church and every other aspect of community life. They build long-term relationships with young people and do everything they can to present the love of Jesus in word and deed – in Bible-speak they live as 'salt' and 'light'.

Today John is involved in this remarkable ministry himself. He runs the EDEN Bus ministry, travelling all over the inner city of Manchester, helping to change the lives of some of the most damaged and vulnerable young people.

For too long much of our Christianity has revolved around a series of meetings as we desperately wait for God to 'fill me up and sort me out'. I sometimes wonder if God is thinking, 'What's the point – if you won't take what I give you and go out to the hurting and the broken on your doorstep?' This is why *Rebuild* is exactly what the church needs. It will help us to get our eyes off ourselves and on to a world in need.

The exciting news about EDEN is that it's working, and bit by bit some of the toughest parts of Manchester are being transformed. If God can do that here, think about what he can do where you are!

A health warning for leaders

Do try this at home

This is a book about action. The sort of action that comes from a little understanding of how God feels about our world, especially the bit of the world we actually live in. This book is about God's deep concern for people, and the challenge of the implications of that for us in our daily lives. This book is about ordinary Christians who have taken that concern of God seriously, and have done something about it where they are. Our aim is to move you and your house group to do likewise.

Always read the label. Don't skip the first part. 'Preparing for action' is about building essential foundations and avoiding painful mistakes. We suggest you study one chapter a week, and encourage your group members to read the 'Food for thought' before meeting together. Then consider the Bible passages together, discuss the questions, pray together, and using the ideas for action and the stories, reflect on how each of you might respond.

Don't try it all at once. The second part, 'Into the community', looks at the different areas of need in our society today. If your home group is beginning to form an idea of what areas of need you might tackle, pick out the relevant chapters and study them together. If you are still uncertain, encourage the group members to read through the book themselves, and to make suggestions. You will see that not every type of need is covered. Space doesn't permit this, and it would be difficult to do justice to the issues involved, but principles can be drawn from similar areas.

Think before you act. Each chapter includes examples of action both to inspire and to inform group members. There are discussion questions with a biblical link, geared towards growing the group's understanding of some of the attitudes and issues surrounding the topic.

Take your time. Some ideas for action are given, along with a checklist of do's and don'ts. Make sure that you give time to discussing these and praying about them in your group. One of them may be a germ of an idea that God wants you or your group to follow up. To help with the follow-up some brief suggestions are given about where you can get further information, advice or help concerning the particular areas of need that you are interested in.

Don't jump the conclusions. The chapter on the relationship between social action and evangelism in community involvement (p. 157) is essential reading, and in itself should stimulate some lively discussion in your group!

Where does the Bible come in?

Although this isn't a typical Bible study book the Bible is essential as the foundation of all that you will consider and, we hope, act upon, as a result of working your way through this book. Church history is littered with the stories of well-meaning, enthusiastic Christians who lost their way, or became totally overwhelmed as they engaged with needs in society around them, because they didn't have strong enough foundations. These can be put in place by being grounded in the word of God and possessing personal vision.

Stirring sermons, emotion evoked by the pain of those around us, or harrowing pictures on our television screens can leave us feeling that we have to do something. Equally, those very same things may leave us paralysed with anxiety about the scale of the problems and the fear of being overwhelmed by them. Others of us may be inoculated against it all, having become personally disconnected by our soap opera culture that reduces human tragedy to no more than something to observe from a distance.

It is for these reasons that any engagement with local community needs on our part must be undergirded by a firm grasp of what God has to say about it all. And this we will find in the pages of the Bible, as with the Holy Spirit's help the truth contained there is made relevant for us in the twenty-first century. Therefore, as you work through this book you should ask God to give you two 'large ears' – one to hear what he has to say about your community, and the other to hear the heartbeat of the needs of that community. It is as those two areas of listening come together that you will be able to act with confidence to make a difference where you are in the name of Jesus.

PART ONE

Preparing for action

God's passion for people

Fran Beckett

Food for thought

Why passion?

God cares about this world and the people in it. He loves the unlovely and unlovable, the ordinary and the extra-ordinary person. He cares that people are oppressed by sin and all its effects. His is not a slushy naïve sentimentalism but a tangible, passionate and active love with an eternal focus: the people he has created. The God we read about in the Bible has a depth of passion, energy and commitment difficult to ignore. The focus of all that feeling is people, ordinary human beings like you and me.

His love radiates from the pages of the Bible. We read of heart-stopping depths of tenderness in the way God deals with people. And the compassion with which he treats those who are 'harassed and helpless' could not fail to move the hardest of attitudes. Jesus exemplified this. Through both his words and lifestyle we see him making radical statements about the inestimable worth of human beings. He treated all persons with respect regardless of age, race, sex, physical condition or economic status.

Jesus taught that his kingdom applies to all of life, transforming human existence and relationships, bringing wholeness, justice and peace. He embodied love and justice, coming to bring good news into a world dominated by

19

discrimination and oppression. Women, refugees, the poor, people with disabilities or disfiguring diseases were devalued and degraded by a society that cared more for outward show than human dignity. The 'untouchables' of the day experienced the affirming, healing power of his touch upon their bodies. The poor and dispossessed received his personal attention when others ignored them. The mentally troubled and demonized found in him someone who saw beyond their problems to the person they once were, and brought them freedom to be that person again. Children too were invited into a place of belonging with Jesus when others saw them merely as a nuisance.

God hates injustice and oppression, wherever it is and whatever shape it takes. The words spoken by prophets like Amos and Nahum are frightening in the white-hot intensity of God's anger against evil. This is no weak insipid God but one with a consuming zeal for holiness and justice, acting powerfully on behalf of downtrodden people. This side of God's character is sometimes easier to forget or to confine to the pages of the Bible. It's something that can make us feel uncomfortable, so we keep it at the margins of our minds. But he refuses to be limited by our discomfort. Instead, he loves us enough to woo and challenge us into the place of seeing the world as he does.

Seeing the world with new eyes

Why does God want us to see the world as he does? Because he has entrusted to us the privilege and responsibility of being co-conspirators with him in the task of its transformation. As Christians we are partners with him, admittedly junior partners, in enabling people to experience at first hand the reality of his revolutionary love for them. That love is the lifeblood he wants to put into our veins for the good of a needy, hurting world.

We are called to live our lives as his children, disciples and friends. Each of these expressions of relationship with him carries within them the certainty of something of his character and concerns rubbing off on us. If that isn't the case then something is wrong! He challenges us to reject preoccupation with our own self-interests, and instead to listen to the poignant heart-cries of the pain of those around us. He calls us to open our eyes to see, ears to hear, and minds to understand what is going on in our communities. And in case we should fear becoming overwhelmed in the process, he reminds us that he is with us and the resources of heaven are at our disposal.

A limited view of God's passion for people, coupled with feelings of helplessness when faced with the sheer immensity of the task of living out God's concerns, can reinforce certain preoccupations for some Christians. Building deeper personal faith and understanding the word of God can subtly be substituted for putting that word in all its fullness into action. For some, issues of personal morality crowd out a wider concern for justice and community in the world around us. Thus issues such as homosexuality in the church take precedence over wider concerns such as poverty, homelessness, racism and social exclusion. The creeping individualism now so prevalent in the twenty-first century Western world is accepted as the norm because our faith is all about 'God and me'. There is little awareness of just how unbiblical a view this is.

Whole-life discipleship

Repeatedly, in both Old and New Testaments believers are called to whole-life discipleship where our relationship with God impacts every area of our lives. No compartmentalized, Sunday-only and midweek home-group living for Christians. What we do, how we relate to others, how we use our time and money, or behave at work or in our neighbourhoods should all bear the imprint of God's character.

The theme that runs throughout the Bible of God's concern for the vulnerable or those getting a raw deal should run through our lives too. This doesn't need to consist of grandiose gestures but should be expressed through our day-to-day living. And it is only out of deepening intimacy with our God that we will find the vision to express his heart for a hurting world. He himself will equip and give us the grace and courage we need for the task.

What does the Bible say?

━━━━━━━━━━━━━━━━━━━━━━━━━━━━━━━━━━━━━

- Read Isaiah 58:2–10 around the group. What attitudes among his people is God challenging here? How might twenty-first century Christians express these same attitudes?

- Then let someone read out Micah 6:8 a couple of times. Explore together what you think it means. In what ways are these two Bible passages similar?

- Now read Acts 10:38. Here Jesus is described as 'doing good'. As a group think of examples of this, and then discuss why he was not just a 'do-gooder' (in the negative sense of the term).

- Round off your discussion together by listing the attitudes Christians would have if they were personally motivated by God's passion for people.

- Then pray together for the group, and individuals within it, to be gripped in a deeper way than ever before by God's passion for people. It may be necessary first to take time to ask for forgiveness for complacency and a lack of interest in the needs of others.

Something else to think about

A woman in need once encountered a well-meaning Christian leader whose reactions reflected his priorities. As a result she wrote this poem and handed it in to an employee of Shelter:

> I was hungry,
>   and you formed a Bible study group to discuss
>   my hunger.
> I was imprisoned,
>   and you crept off quietly to your chapel and
>   prayed for my release

I was naked,
> and in your mind you debated the morality of my
> appearance.

I was sick,
> and you knelt and thanked God for your health.

I was homeless,
> and you preached to me of the spiritual shelter of
> the love of God.

I was lonely,
> and you left me to pray for me.

You seem so holy, so close to God,
> but I am still very hungry – and lonely – and cold.

Serving Asia's poor

We have much to learn from Christians around the world about the costliness as well as the positive results of coming alongside people at their point of need. One example is that of an organization called Servants to Asia's Poor. They send small teams to live and work in the poorest slums, identifying with people in practical ways. In Cambodia, Christian workers have been focusing on communities who are affected by the most severe HIV epidemic in Asia. Living with the families and supporting them in their acute suffering through providing care for their children, employment training opportunities, and working more widely with disabled children, they are making a welcome difference in the name of Christ. To live in conditions without proper sanitation or clean running water, or in cramped, very basic accommodation, is costly but the rewards of giving hope to those who previously had none make it all worth while.

Salt and light

Fran Beckett

Food for thought

Our television screens are regularly filled with scenes of human misery, and tragic stories jostle for space in the newspaper columns. Bad news captures the headlines, and good news seldom gets more than luke-warm coverage, if it's likely to feature at all. Consequently, a kind of fatigue or even immunity builds up inside us so that we cease to be moved by the evil in the world.

Facing the challenge

Sometimes we hear sermons that stir us deeply, challenging us about the needs of society around us, and how we can make a difference. Stories of seeming 'super-Christians' who give up everything to serve Christ in desperate situations around the world mix a cocktail of feelings such as guilt, fear and doubts as to whether this could ever be for us. Caring projects run by Christian organizations, or even by our churches, reassure us, however, that someone is doing something in the name of Jesus. And so we sit back with relief, and the challenge of those sermons or of what we've heard on the news fades into the background.

Maybe that's not us though. Perhaps we've had a go at getting involved in supporting people who are struggling with life. However, it has gone horribly wrong. They expected more of us than we felt able to give; their problems threatened to drown us, and we just couldn't cope. It was all too much, especially given the pressures and demands of our own lives. Anyway, they didn't seem interested in what we tried to tell them about their need for salvation. So we pulled out, and from now on are going to ensure that we don't get in over our heads again.

The thing is, both of the reactions described above are understandable. They are also, not surprisingly, quite prevalent among Christians, although we may not want to admit it for ourselves. On the other hand, some people reading this may be seeking to live out in their everyday lives the truth of God's passion for people. Life has its ups and downs, its heartaches and joys, but you're hanging in there. For you, a little encouragement would go a long way.

Well, here it comes: you're certainly on the right track! The Bible is packed with references regarding God's concern for justice and righteousness; in fact there are over eight hundred. Repeatedly, God speaks of his heart for those on the margins of society and calls his people to be instruments of support, healing and transformation. Our voices, faces, hands and lives make his love tangible and more accessible to those who are hurting in some way.

Right where we are

Our availability is the key. As we go about our daily lives we encounter people all the time. Standing in supermarket checkout queues or at the school gates, on our journeys to work and in the workplace itself, down our streets and in shopping centres we interact with people. 'Neighbour', 'relative', 'work colleague', 'friend' and 'passing acquaintance' are some of the labels they carry in our minds. Each person has a unique set of life circumstances, and each, whether he or she acknowledges it or not, has a need for a personal relationship with the God who loves individuals more than words can express. As we are available and interact with people the possibility opens up for them to access God's love for themselves.

Each of us has a distinct 'life neighbourhood' – a set of

relationships, circumstances and geography unique to us. For some of us it may mean that the bulk of our time is spent in the workplace; while others seldom go further than the end of their road.

Wherever we spend our time and whatever the collection of people we encounter, we have the opportunity in some form to make God's love more accessible to those around us. Jesus talked about those who follow him being 'salt' and 'light' in the world. Salt brings flavour into the lives of those for whom everything has become tasteless, grey and depressing. It acts to prevent decay and destruction of relationships in families and communities, and is a preservative, affirming and working for that which is wholesome in people's lives. Light brings hope and relief into the darkness that threatens to overwhelm because of poverty or mental illness. Light that points the way to reconciliation in relationships, and true human worth whether disabled, older in years, an ex-prisoner or a single parent. And light that illuminates the truth about God and his passion for people, irrespective of our messed-up lives and resistance to him.

Christians in the Western world often talk about the pressures of modern living. It can be a struggle to balance long working hours with family responsibilities and involvement in the church. Exhaustion from keeping it all going is common, and along with that comes withdrawal into a private life that leaves little space for engagement with others outside the immediate circle. Exhortations to get involved in the community can therefore create an unease, a sense of guilt, but no action save that of giving some money so that others can run the necessary projects.

To stop at this is to succumb to a project mentality, a view that somehow the way in which we live our lives is irrelevant as long as someone is demonstrating the compassion of Christ on our behalf. The thing is, the Bible is quite clear that *all* followers of Jesus are to be salt and light. No opt-outs, and no time off for good behaviour! Rather than get overburdened by guilt we can ask God to help us be salt and light right where we are. If we were to do this some radical, and probably unexpected, results would follow.

The Bible repeatedly emphasizes 'whole life' discipleship. There is no room for compartmentalized Christian living, where being a Christian only applies to our personal relationship with God and our church life. The presence of Jesus in us and with us should spill over wherever we go. This doesn't necessarily mean using holy language, or stressing our distinctiveness as Christians in a way that makes us unattractive and inaccessible to others, but can simply be a smile or a genuinely listening ear. Sometimes costly, committed action will be needed, motivated by love for the God who sacrificed himself for lost humankind.

What does the Bible say?

- Read Galatians 5:15 together a couple of times. Give the group members paper and pencils and ask them to draw a picture or diagram of who they consider their neighbours to be. Then go around the group sharing the pictures.

- Then read around together Matthew 5:13–16. Discuss what being salty might look like in
  (1) the neighbourhood in which the church is situated;
  (2) group members' 'life neighbourhoods'.

- What would the opposite look like, that is 'if the salt loses its saltiness'? Make sure you are practical and rooted in everyday life in your discussion.

- Consider together what you think about the idea in Matthew 5:16 of letting others see the good deeds you do. Isn't this just boastful or pushy?

- And then look at Colossians 4:5, 6. Explore what it means to have one's conversation 'seasoned with salt'.

How might this fit with engaging with the pressures and needs of those around us?

- Finally, return to the pictures drawn at the beginning. Have a few moments' silence in which group members are encouraged to lay their pictures before God, asking him whether there's anything he wants them to do about the people they have drawn. Then have a time of thanksgiving for God's love, and prayer for the group to grow in effectiveness as salt and light.

Ideas for action

- If you're collecting your children from school, arrive early so there's time to talk to other parents who are waiting.
- Ask God to give you relevant questions to ask the people you see regularly, so that you will begin to know them better.
- Try smiling instead of frowning.
- When you ask someone how they are, expect an answer.
- Think about simple, practical ways in which to show your work colleagues that you value them.
- Perhaps on the way to work you can pray for those in your church who remain in the local community most of the time that they would be effective there as salt and light.
- Any new neighbours? Take them a bunch of flowers, a smile and a welcome to the neighbourhood, and an offer of assistance should they ever need it.

Workplace action projects in Rome

In Rome, some Christians have formed several groups in their workplace to initiate social action projects and centres of reconciliation. Because of the nature of their jobs the bulk of their time is spent away from their local communities. Instead of this leading to their becoming disengaged from the needs of Italian society they have decided to start where they are and make a difference through building on the strengths that already exist. These include their working relationships, the opportunities to get together easily to plan and to pray, and their access to work-based resources. Using lunchtimes and evenings they have got involved in serving the people they pass every day on their way into the office, many of them poor, homeless and struggling with life. They also make sure that they remain involved in their local churches, who in turn pray for them and support them.

3

Listeners first

Fran Beckett

Food for thought

In the midst of the rush and bustle of life, taking time to listen in depth can seem like a luxury. The drive towards achievement, filling our days with busyness or preoccupation with survival brings a deafness to the voices around and inside us. Yet, if we are serious about embracing God's passion for people in some way then making space for listening is vital. And to be increasingly effective as salt and light where we are day by day we must 'hear' what is going on around us.

The voices inside

Sounds fine in theory but what does it actually mean, and what are we supposed to be listening to? Yes, we need to listen to others, but we also need to listen to what God is saying. Furthermore, we need to listen to ourselves. If we are serious about bringing the love and goodness of God into the world around us we must have a growing awareness of what we're like.

The time has come for a vigorous reappraisal of our own attitudes, prejudices and fears. Not an exercise in introspection, but a prayerful assessment of who and what we are, and what by God's grace we can become. Nor should it be an exercise merely to make us feel better –

although greater wholeness through coming afresh to the cross of Christ can be a glorious by-product. Rather, it is a process to bring insight and create space for God to change us into people who powerfully 'incarnate' his love.

Boxes and pigeon holes

If we're going to get more involved with people the truth is that few people have uncomplicated lives. Even the most apparently straightforward situations will often hide a tangled mess. And it's when we encounter this that our feelings can start to react. Prejudice is a powerful force, not always easily recognizable in ourselves. Usually we identify it more easily in others. Most of us regard with sneaking suspicion or outright dislike certain individuals or groups of people. Perhaps these are people with a lot of money, or those receiving social security payments – the stereotypical view being that the former are callous and self-indulgent, while the latter are irresponsible scroungers. Some of us have an aversion to assertive women, practising homosexuals, people from a different ethnic background to ours, a political party, or particular characteristics in an individual. Reactions like these must be dealt with before we can reach out in love to others. We all need God's searchlight to examine and deal with us (Psalm 139:23, 24).

One way of coping with prejudice or fear is by being patronizing: the feeling of somehow being superior, being more together as a person, that spills over into how we talk about and to other people, like sarcastic humour that is always quick to highlight the weaknesses of others. Reducing people to labels or pigeon-holing them as problems dehumanizes them, and makes a mockery of the gospel. Attitudes like these will only be counteracted as we grow in awareness of the powerful grace of God. It is experience of that grace and recognition of our own frailties that enables humility, and stimulates a kind of holy awe as we look upon the wonder of another human being carrying, however marred, the stamp of God's image.

Pink-tinted shades

Sentimentality is another poor attitude to have when dealing with people and their needs, and is to be avoided in any form. It is a superficial attitude that fails to face the potentially demanding nature of getting involved with other human beings. For example, a sentimental person gushes over a golden-haired child in a wheelchair but is later repelled by the basic necessity of changing her incontinence pads. In Jesus we see no trace of sentimentality. No rose-coloured spectacles for him. No disillusionment with people, because he has no illusions in the first place – he knows all there is to know, and still loves us.

Goosebumps and all that

The other thing we need to listen to is our fears. Fear is powerful, as it can paralyse action and reinforce apathy. There is a risk of being overwhelmed and unable to cope with human problems, and deprivation and personal pain are never tidy. They tend to spill out all over the place, often refusing to fit into neat categories, formulas and solutions.

Some Christians fear not so much the scale of need as the fear of somehow being contaminated by it. A healthy caution is valuable, but we must remember that we are sent into the world as Jesus was sent into the world (John 17:15–18). Perhaps also, our fear of venturing into the morass of human sinfulness has blinded us to how far the world's values have crept into the church. Power, self-interest and status can preoccupy us, while buildings and traditions may matter more than people. A far cry from the kingdom values taught and modelled by Jesus.

A sense of personal inadequacy, of being ill equipped and inexperienced, is a fear many have. Being realistic about our limitations is essential, but to believe that we are stuck with them is not. Recognition of a lack of experience can be a springboard for change. Maybe someone older (or younger!) and wiser can support or mentor us. Or we can find help through reading, visiting specialist Websites, or by gaining training. We should never promise someone more than we can offer, or somehow see ourselves as 'the rescuer' in a difficult situation. And when we take our fears and inadequacies to God, coupled with a willingness to take risks with him, new possibilities previously only dreamt of can open up.

Listening to others

Sensitivity to others is important. What do you feel like when you're trying to tell someone something important and it's obvious they're not listening to you? There's a glazed expression in their eyes, or they're vigorously practising the 'rubber neck syndrome', looking around and past you while you're talking because they're trying to catch someone else's attention! The message in those circumstances comes across loudly and clearly: you don't matter.

We may not be social workers, psychiatrists or vicars. We may not have all the answers, but pathways to change sometimes open up when we are prepared to listen to and unconditionally accept the person talking to us.

Being sensitive to people involves a growing ability to understand their situation and pain, to have the capacity to identify by standing alongside, offering support – and standing back when it's appropriate. Sensitive Christians have the compassion of Jesus, but avoid getting so sucked in that the boundary between their feelings and those of the hurting person becomes unrecognizable. Also, we should not impose our solutions, but enable people to explore options and make their own choices.

It's your serve

The language of servanthood in the Bible can seem quaint or irrelevant in these days of management gurus, assertiveness training, and performance targets. Jesus, however, came among people to serve them, and Christians are called to be like this too. This is not the same as being a 'doormat', taken advantage of and trampled upon by others. True service involves consideration of the needs and interests of those with whom we come into contact. It means treating people with dignity whatever their circumstances or station in life. It includes putting ourselves out for them in such a way that their range of life choices is extended, and not so that they become overly dependent upon us. On the contrary, they should be empowered to exercise responsibility for their own lives and relationships.

Stickability

We live in an instant age – from instant meals to instant access to the other side of the world through our computer screens. Turn on the tap and we expect, if we live in one of the richer nations of the world, water to come gushing out. Relationships, however, are not instant, and years of being treated badly or long experiences of loneliness are not usually cancelled out in a moment. Service of others includes 'stickability', a willingness to go on even if someone isn't grateful or particularly cooperative. Service of others involves reliability – being and doing what we have committed ourselves to. That can be tough sometimes, especially if this is tested by those whose previous experience is that of always being let down. God himself is totally and eternally reliable. He is utterly consistent and is never swayed by irrational whims or moods. He keeps his promises and helps us both to make wise promises, and to keep them.

What does the Bible say?

* Start your time together by praying, asking God to help you to be good listeners to him and to each other as you discuss the questions.

* Take turns around the group giving 'feeling' type words to describe the experience of *not* being listened to. Write them on a large piece of paper and hold it up for all to see. Then briefly take turns again describing instead how it feels to *be* listened to.

* Get different group members to read out Proverbs

18:13 and Proverbs 25:20. What are the links between these verses, and why do you think they are so strongly stated?

• Getting involved with people in caring action can be a scary business. Read 1 John 4:18, and explore together how this might apply when engaging with individual and community needs.

• Read Luke 10:27–37. In pairs, explore what you think each of the main players in this familiar story of 'the Good Samaritan' was feeling. Try to imagine yourself in their situation. Then identify and list the attitudes that probably lay behind those feelings. Next, each of the pairs should give feedback: one answer under feelings and another under attitudes. Take turns doing this until the full range discussed has been covered. Consider together what you've heard. What application do these issues have for you as twenty-first century Christians in your particular setting?

• End the time by praying for each other in small groups, sharing any attitudes you struggle with or areas which you would like to develop.

• Close by reminding the group through reading out together Ephesians 3:20, 21 what God is able to do.

Something else to think about

James was an accountant, highly successful in his job and generally respected in his local church for his sound business sense. Trevor worked as a hospital porter. He was in the same church as James but stayed more in the background. Obviously ill at ease in large groups his hesitant manner contrasted strongly with James's confident, outspoken style.

The church had recently come into contact with a young family struggling with financial and housing problems. It seemed sensible that James should use his expertise to advise them. Accordingly, he arranged an appointment for them to see him at his office. They arrived late and throughout the interview the family hardly uttered a word. Despite this, James swiftly and efficiently worked out a housekeeping budget. He rebuked them for spending too much money on 'unhealthy' food, and then ushered them out of the office with the promise of further help should they need it.

After this, they continued spasmodically to attend the church but seemed to avoid James. So, with a shrug of the shoulders he assumed that they'd taken his professional advice and did nothing more about them.

Meanwhile, feeling rather nervous, Trevor called in to see them at their flat. He sat playing with the children, drinking tea out of a chipped mug, and offered to help to find a job for the husband through his contacts at the hospital. He visited regularly, often hesitant in his manner but always prepared to listen and lend a hand. He helped them gradually redecorate the flat, and after several months managed to put the husband in touch with a suitable job.

Outwardly, James had what was needed to assist that family but his attitudes let him down. Outwardly, Trevor had little to offer but he was the one who actually showed the love of Jesus in action!

Finding a focus

Fran Beckett

Food for thought

The previous two chapters have concentrated mainly on people as individuals. Indeed, many Christians when they think about social action or some form of caring activity see this almost exclusively as being about individual needs. There is no doubt that individuals are important to God, however, just to concentrate on a single person is to miss a vital factor, that of the importance of community. For surrounding every person is a network, a web of relationships, that affects their lives in one way or another.

More than a bunch of individuals

Human beings were created to be in relationship, connected with their God, fellow human beings, and the environment. Right at the beginning of the Bible, God states that it's not good for a person to be alone (Genesis 2:18). And from that point on we see a community of people growing up around the first man and woman.

As the story of God's people unfurls in the Bible the notion of community can be found throughout. Early in their history God states his commitment to build them as a community (Genesis 48:4). Repeatedly he deals with his people and the surrounding nations as whole communities. The Israelites are referred to as a community and are usually collectively held accountable to God. The link between people in community is assumed as we see whole tribes being affected by the sin or blessing of one person.

Communities are portrayed as places of belonging and sources of help when in need. The community is regarded as having a collective responsibility towards those on its margins, drawing them in and including them in the benefits of community life. There were strict injunctions from God for compassion, generosity and justice to characterize how his people were to go about relating to one another and working together. There was a recognition that, human frailty being what it is, this wouldn't always work out as God intended. A means of rebalancing and reordering communal life was therefore introduced through the year of Jubilee (Leviticus 25). Intensely practical, this had implications for land and property rights, possession of wealth, and other matters such as employment status. Undergirding it all was an understanding that relationships between people were to be based on mutual respect, on our treating others as God treats them.

Perhaps even more important than all this, however, is the community at the heart of the Godhead. Vast theological tomes have been written on the doctrine of the Trinity, illustrating how wonderful, yet beyond human comprehension, the fact of Father, Son and Holy Spirit as one God is. This is not the place to attempt to explain this amazing truth about our God. However, what is clear is that each member of the Godhead fulfils a distinct yet complementary function. There is an individuality and yet such mutuality, harmony and unity of relationship between the three that they are one. Here we see perfect community at work.

Community now

Christians in the Western world have often emphasized a rather individualistic and private approach to personal faith. This is not the same in other parts of the world, where cultures have a strong sense of community relationships built on interdependence and belonging. In such places the church as a community and Christians as active members of their local communities are taken for granted.

In Britain there have been a number of Government initiatives to promote a more integrated society, with strategies for neighbourhood renewal being pursued in an attempt to turn around the sense of disconnectedness of many people. In America the phenomenon of 'the singleton society' has been highlighted through growing numbers of young people having no relationship at all with their surrounding community. Bonds are formed instead in Internet chat rooms and with narrow bands of people with similar interests and backgrounds.

The coalition of over sixty British national and regional Christian organizations, named REBUILD, who have written this book are committed to a biblical vision to see local communities rebuilt. The fact that there is a church, as well as a pub, in most neighbourhoods is not a coincidence. Christians are uniquely placed both with a vision and a presence to be able to make a positive impact, not just in the lives of individuals but also in whole communities. Where community is eroding or breaking down Christians have a vital role to play.

Being sent as Jesus was

At the beginning of John's Gospel we read how Jesus came into the world. One version describes it as him 'moving into our neighbourhood'. We see in Jesus a breathtaking and almost shocking identification with human beings. The God of the universe contracted into the body of a tiny baby born into a rural peasant family. Growing up in ignominy, followed by a motley crowd of society's misfits and those without power or status, and then dying a criminal's death on a cross. And then we read later in John's Gospel (17:18) that we are sent into the world like he was!

Jesus was always to be found with people. He invested in relationships; he had time for those whom others brushed aside; he rubbed shoulders with the unlovely and didn't hold himself at a distance expecting to be treated as someone with earthly status or power. In fact he had harsh words for the religious leaders who, nose in the air, distanced themselves from ordinary people. If we are sent into the world as Jesus was we have to make room for people in our lives, rejecting the individualistic, self-absorbed culture of our day.

Small but significant

We need to remember that the community around us doesn't necessarily see the local church or Christians in as positive a light as we do. Their experience may be of blocked driveways or cars obstructing pavements on a Sunday morning. Equally, they may have had their Friday nights disturbed by rowdy teenagers spilling out of the church youth club. Or their favourite soap opera might have been interrupted by a couple of earnest people on their doorstep telling them they were doomed unless they became Christians. None of these negative encounters is the best introduction to the vibrant adventure of new life in Christ!

For Christians, involvement in the community doesn't need to be about grandiose projects. As individuals we may not touch the lives of huge numbers of people. None the less, a desire to see neighbourliness grow and your locality become a friendlier, safer place is something that God wants too. You can therefore pray and invest your energies into this with confidence. We can all make a difference merely with a smile, a greeting, showing interest in the lives of others, volunteering to help those with needs, getting involved in arranging a street party or setting up a Neighbourhood Watch scheme. The possibilities are endless, and will vary greatly according to the sort of neighbourhood we live in.

Prayer brings focus

By this stage you may be thinking, 'It was hard enough considering how to be more loving towards a few other people, but now she's suggesting that I somehow tackle the whole of my neighbourhood!' Yes, a daunting task because of its sheer scale and complexity, and of course there's a huge difference between an inner-city housing estate, a far-flung rural community or a sedate seaside town, let along all the variations in between. The question remains: where do we start?

Think about this quotation by George Bernard Shaw, who wasn't a Christian but none the less understood the importance of vision: 'You see things as they are and ask "why?" but I dream things that never were and ask "why not?"' The place to start is with a sense of God's immensity, and that he is the God of the 'why not?' Take time to walk around your area, praying as you go that he would give you his heart and insights into what the community is like. Get a map of the neighbourhood, mark the places where local people regularly go, such as pubs, the health centre, local shops, and so on. Then pray about those places and what goes on in them. Start praying regularly for the local police, social workers, doctors and your local council members and officials.

Communities can be changed through prayer but we are also called to engage in action. As you pray, you will get a clearer idea of what to do. There will always be things attracting your attention, but as you pray about your neighbours, contacts and wider community you will find a God-directed focus for action. Where do you start? Right where you are. Begin praying, and make efforts to grow in understanding of what is going on locally; then test your thinking against the opinion of those whom you respect. And if you still have no clear focus, simply ask God to bring people across your path to whom he wants you to show the love of Jesus.

What does the Bible say?

- Prepare for your time together by getting a detailed map of the area and some coloured pins or coloured sticky dots to put on the map. When people arrive ask them to assist in building up a picture of the neighbourhood by highlighting on the map the places people regularly go. Include where group members live, churches and other places of worship, shops, pubs, hospitals, health centres, surgeries, community centres, police stations, council offices, and so on.

• Remind people that each locality will be made up of a number of distinct types of community: people of a common background or identity, people coming together to share a common interest, and people living in the same geographical area. In the light of this, are there any additional comments group members want to make about the map before you? What are the barriers between the different communities? (They may be physical such as a main road; or they may be attitudes, or language, and so on.) What is the community like?

• Then pray asking God to give you insight into how he views the area.

• Read Jeremiah 29:7 and then Revelation 21:3–5. These give a glorious picture of the new future that God is working to bring into being. What are the main themes in the descriptions in these verses? If they were to be applied to the community on the map before you, how different would that community be?

• Discuss the 'Ideas for action' section below. Then read Nehemiah 2:12. Nehemiah was in the beginning stages of a life-changing project. For him it was important to know 'what God had put' in his heart 'to do'. Pray together for a similar experience as a group and as individuals.

Ideas for action

Discuss how you as a group can get to know the community better, and decide what to do. There are various possibilities listed here, and you may be able to think of others.

- Get people in the group and in your church who are involved in some sort of community activity or project to tell the group about it.
- At each group meeting have a copy of the local newspaper to discuss and pray about the contents.
- Arrange a series of low-key prayer walks around the neighbourhood.
- Ask a couple of the group members to find out what opportunities for voluntary work there are in the neighbourhood by contacting the local Council for Voluntary Service or similar organizations.
- Obtain the names of senior police officers or your local councillors and start praying for them regularly as a group.
- Get together with other groups in the church and arrange a special meeting to invite the leader of the council or your MP to give their views on the needs of the community and the possible role of the church.
- Put together a simple public questionnaire on the needs of the community, and arrange for the findings to be put in the local paper. (Note that this will raise expectations that you're going to take action in light of the findings!)
- Keep the map you've worked on, add photos, and have it on display at each group meeting.

Prayer transforming community

In 1994 the Redeemed Church of God sensed a call to draw members of the black majority churches together to pray. Accordingly, twice a year ten thousand people from black majority churches come together at the London Arena for a night of prayer, the Festival of Light. The evenings include times of praise as well as prayer for different aspects of government depending on what is topical at the time, and for community groups such as the police. Also, on the first Friday of every month, a hundred people meet in an auditorium in Croydon for the Night of Destiny prayer group. Members of churches and home groups come together to pray around the theme of transforming the community. Prayer might focus on topical issues, local government elections, or acceptance of the black community and that they might find favour in what they do.

Working together

Sometimes we can achieve a lot more by being prepared to work together with others. And sometimes we can open the door to others getting involved. This story provides a powerful illustration.

A Government initiative was recently launched with the aim of using small, local community groups to deliver introductory information technology training to local people. The Vines Centre Trust, an established Christian charity with experience in assisting unemployed people to gain new skills, presented the possibility to the network of churches in Medway, Kent, of running an 'ICT Learning Centre'. Vines Centre Trust offered to act as lead partner in making the bid and taking responsibility for ongoing accountability and monitoring. They received a positive response from four potential partners. A successful bid was made to set up five centres, based in one rural and two urban churches, in a high-street drop-in for young people run by Youth for Christ and one at the Trust's own base. Working together will enable the partners to employ a manager and to provide technical support to all five centres. Not only will they be able to share resources and expertise but the lives of many more people will be touched than would otherwise have been possible.

Where angels fear to tread: preparing for action

Jill Garner

Sometimes Christians in their enthusiasm for neighbourhood action 'rush in where angels fear to tread'. In this
chapter we will look at how to avoid misguided or short-
lived zeal and how to engage in social action that is rooted
in God, meeting real needs and with lasting effects.

Angels appear in the Bible as God's agents, which is what
we want to be through our social action. Sometimes they
have a message from God, reassuring people by telling
them not to be afraid. Most famously they brought good
news of peace on earth – news of restoration and wholeness,
of Jesus living among us. Sometimes angels are unrecog-
nized; they seem to move about without anyone realizing
they are there doing God's work. That's part of our role in
our neighbourhoods too. Sometimes we are to get on
quietly with God's work, without recognition but safe in the
knowledge that we are his agents.

Finally, we know angels are part of a spiritual realm. By
prayer, praise, worship, intercession and with spiritual
disciplines such as fasting, we too engage with spiritual
forces as part of living out God's love in our neighbourhoods.

In angels' footsteps

Look at these three references to angels:

> But the angel said to them, 'Do not be afraid. I bring you good news of great joy that will be for all the people. Today in the town of David a Saviour has been born to you; he is Christ the Lord' (Luke 2:10).

> Do not forget to entertain strangers, for by so doing some people have entertained angels without knowing it (Hebrews 13:2).

> For our struggle is not against flesh and blood, but against the rulers, against the authorities, against the powers of this dark world and against the spiritual forces of evil in the heavenly realms (Ephesians 6:12).

Which do you find most exciting and why? The one you responded to most warmly may give you a clue to the most effective way for you to work in your neighbourhood.

At the Cephas Project in Huddersfield a group of churches work together to run a Lighthouse Centre, which includes a community print shop and detached youth work. These activities are supported by a group of older people who pray for the work. Different people are fulfilling different but equally important roles. Some are in the background supporting through prayer, others give regular time to the project, and others are out on the streets working directly with teenagers. Christians are bringing good news, working in an unassuming way and engaging in prayer, and in this way treading in angels' footsteps.

The social-action journey

The Shaftesbury Society, the national Christian social action organization, uses the idea of a social-action journey to help churches or groups of churches to think about how they engage in their community. From experience we have learned that time spent in the early stages of the social-action journey is well spent. If we're activists by nature we'll want to get on with doing something. It is important to resist the temptation to hurry, however, even though there can be pressure to get something started. Time spent at the beginning means that there will be less muddle, misunderstanding, and missing of the mark later on.

The social-action journey

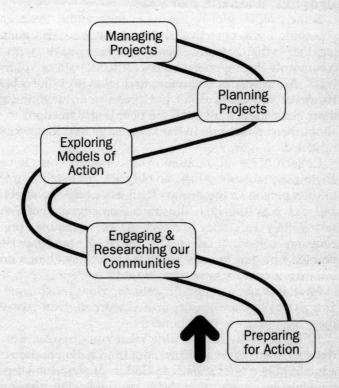

Your church may already have done something like this, or you may like to consider how your home group could follow a similar journey. The rest of this chapter will help you explore ways of setting out that are rooted in God and will last.

We can only start from where we are. The following activities are to help you think about your present situation.

Skills audit

You may either just be starting to think about social action, or are already involved. You may or may not know each other well. It doesn't matter. Think about what you have to offer in working with others to serve God through some kind of social action in your area.

Some people refer to this as a 'skills audit'. As a group you could list the practical skills of members. Also, consider together what natural links members have with the community through neighbours, contacts, paid or voluntary work. A fun way of beginning to do this is outlined below. However you do it, don't put pressure on anyone to say more than they want to. Give people the freedom to talk about themselves, safe in the knowledge that they won't be ridiculed.

Collect items at random from around your house – anything is suitable: a fork, an old sock … Give one or more to each person in the group. Then ask people to select one and say how the item illustrates something about themselves they can offer the group. For example, on one occasion someone selected a piece of sandpaper and pointed out that he was good at smoothing things down, but that he could also be abrasive at times!

Next talk about your limitations. How much time can you give? What are your fears and worries? Don't dwell on these but recognize them honestly.

Find some way of recording what you discover. You can write it down, draw a picture, put it on a flip chart or make a model. Then offer it back to God in prayer, thanking him for what he's given you. Now have ready to give out to group members a picture of a tree. It should be large and have a lot of branches on it. Ask people to reflect quietly for a few minutes on where they see themselves on the journey of faith and action that this book has taken them on so far. Get them to draw themselves on the tree as a picture of where they are and how they feel about it all. Then share drawings together in pairs or with the wider group, depending on how confident with each other the group members are.

Researching the community

In Shaftesbury we emphasize understanding the community and its needs and resources. It's all too easy to rush in with good ideas of what you think is needed, but by doing this you can make things worse. You can take control, respect and hope away from the very people you want to serve. That wasn't Jesus' way. He dwelt among us and

> did not consider equality with God something to be
>   grasped,
> but made himself nothing
>   taking the form of a servant.
>
> (Philippians 2:6–7)

Can you think of a time when someone made decisions that affected your life without talking to you about it? How did you feel?

Often people feel they know what the needs of an area are and have ideas of what should be done. For instance, a church might decide to set up a youth club without taking the time to find out what the young people think about this, or what their interests and needs are. Equally, perhaps there are already a number of similar activities catered for in the area, making the need for another club unnecessary.

It is important to speak to the young people first, as they will feel far more positive towards the scheme if they have had the opportunity to become involved in it. It becomes their project rather than something imposed on them.

What do you know about the area you live in? How can you find out more? Think of people you can talk to or places

49

you can go for information. Remember that by starting to ask people what they think and consulting those involved in the community you will begin to raise expectations. So beware of making lots of initial noise through your research activity followed by a deafening silence!

Also, remember that people often see the church as irrelevant, or they stereotype us as only being interested in 'converting' people. Therefore, they may regard our enquiries initially with some suspicion. The language we use is therefore vital.

Your town hall or library can be a good place to start. They will have information drawn from the last official census on the local-population mix, documents that outline the council's priorities and plans for dealing with social need, and lists of community organizations. Local radio and newspapers can also be a good source of anecdotal information about the community, as well as about what groups and activities exist. Also, remember that other churches may already have done something like this and so may have information that they can pass on to you without your having to start from scratch.

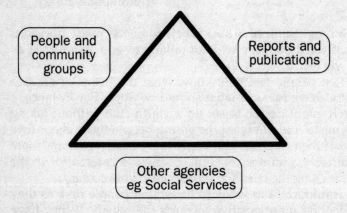

Draw this triangle on a large piece of paper. Ask people for ideas of sources of information and list them beside the three sides.

Now think what questions you might like to ask. What do you want to find out about? How will you shape the questions?

The next thing to think about is who can ask the questions or do the research, and when can they begin? Time spent on research is important, because without it you are unlikely to meet people's needs. Also, the process of researching helps to build relationships and involves people, giving them respect and a voice in the community. It means that those who benefit from the subsequent action have some control over it and will be more likely to help keep it going.

Keeping in touch with God is vital as you carry out this research. One way to do this is to follow a cycle of action, reflection and prayer, as shown in the illustration below. Keep going around the circle as you move forward on your social-action journey.

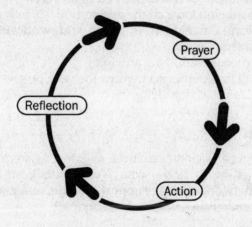

What next?

The next stage of the social-action journey is to think of what you can do – models of action – as a result of what you have learnt so far. Perhaps a one-off or short-term activity, or something longer term? What type of activity and to whom will it be geared? Why are you doing it and what do you hope to achieve? Should you get involved in something that is already going on, or start your own activity? The following chapters will help you think about some of these issues and the subsequent stages of the journey.

Do's and don'ts

- Do be open: to God, to people, to being surprised at what God will do.
- Do be creative: dream dreams, be bold.
- Do be patient: it will take time and there may be disappointments. Be patient with yourself too and be realistic about what you can manage.
- Do be alongside: work with people.
- Do be challenging: don't just accept things as they are.
- Do be yourself: God will use you as you are.
- Don't think you have all the answers.
- Don't forget that God is already at work in your community.
- Don't ignore what others are doing.
- Don't fail to consult and involve the very people you're seeking to get alongside.

Further help

The Shaftesbury Society produces a guide to community research ('Getting to Know your Neighbours'), an Action for Change network offering support, training and materials to churches and groups involved in social action:

The Shaftesbury Society
Church Development Services
16 Kingston Road
London SW19 1JZ
Tel: 020 8239 5555
Website: www.shaftesburysoc.org.uk

Tearfund has a training process and pack ('Church, Community and Change') for use with local churches:

Tearfund
100 Church Road
Teddington TW11 8QE
Tel: 020 8977 9144
Website: www.tearfund.org.uk

Christian Action Networks (CANs) unite churches engaged in social action in geographical areas:

CANs
c/o Evangelical Alliance
Whitefield House
186 Kennington Park Road
London SE11 4BT
Tel: 020 8207 2152
Website: www.eauk.org/cans

Churches' Community Work Alliance (CCWA) initiates, supports and encourages community work in the life of churches:

CCWA
24 Tynesdale Close
Wylam
Newcastle upon Tyne
NE41 8EX
Website: www.ccwa.org.uk

PART TWO

Into the community

Neighbourhood impact

Mannie Stewart

It's a sunny Sunday in June and Christine is about to leave for a day out with her two young sons. She's heard about a 'family fun day' at a park in the town centre. 'Yes, Mum; let's go. It's brill!' exclaims one excited child. 'All right, that's settled then,' she says, pleased to have found something that the boys want to do.

Arriving at the park, Christine discovers that the event is run by a local church. Mildly surprised by this, she nonetheless finds a friendly atmosphere and free activities: a bouncy castle, face painting, penalty shoot-outs for the energetic, and live music playing on a nearby stage. Christine and the boys have a great time and she makes friends with the organizers. Later she discovers they have a parent-and-toddler group which her younger son can attend, and a football league for the older soccer-mad one.

The members of Hoole Baptist Church, along with a few others, have organized the fun day, as they have done for the past few years. This year they decided to run the event in conjunction with REBUILD's 'Community Week' initiative.

Community weeks provide a way for churches to increase their involvement with their neighbourhood. They encourage the running of small events or initiatives that serve the community in practical ways. They also provide those of us who don't work full-time for the church with a way of getting involved in community outreach.

In this book, other chapters give examples of how sustained community involvement is needed to build quality relationships and to reap both social and spiritual results. This chapter needs to be taken in context along with these others. We need to find a way of making a start, however, and the 'Community Week' approach is helpful. Although this approach has many benefits, below just five are listed.

It's visible

What impression do people in your neighbourhood have about your church? Do they even know it exists? Perhaps you have a highly attractive and visible building, or maybe one that is run down, or no building at all. How then is your local community aware of your presence among them?

The UK Evangelical Alliance carried out a survey of its member churches a few years back. It asked two key questions. The first was, 'Do you believe in a holistic gospel?' The answer was 'Yes' from 80% of the churches. The second question asked if churches thought that people in their neighbourhood considered the church to be relevant to them. Only 20% of churches answered 'Yes' to this question! Whatever your church building looks like, it is only by church members finding ways of *meeting* and *serving* people in the neighbourhood that true impressions can be formed.

Andy is the minister at the Baptist Church in Hoole. He believes that to gain this visibility churches need to build healthy relationships and serve people with gladness. The local authority have seen the church fun days and have been so impressed that it grants the necessary permits with ease, and now even wants to run joint events with them. The local press too has been supportive and their coverage has meant that, after just three events, the fun day has now been adopted as an annual community event.

Discuss at this point in your group what part you think Christians should play in creating opportunities for celebration within the community. Consider together the implications of what Jesus both taught and did, as described in Luke 14:12–24; 5:29–39. Are there any others clues in the Bible about the importance of community celebration?

It's manageable

It's easy to fall into the trap of thinking that making an impact on your neighbourhood equals big projects costing lots of money. Some things will of course fall into this category, but there is wide scope to have a significant impact with small-scale initiatives. A church in the East Midlands takes a small group of older widows and widowers out to an evening meal once in a while. These people do not need money, but they would be desperately lonely without these nights out. They dress up to the nines, enjoy an evening together, and are very grateful to the church that organizes it.

In order for these events to be manageable, however, church leaders cannot be expected to be solely responsible for them. Although the church in Hoole has a small group of people organizing their fun day, when the event is on, around 80% of the church members become involved in some way – which makes most of the church a part of the success of these events.

It meets needs

Angela (not her real name) from Derby could take it no longer! Her daughter's car kept being broken into. She had prayed with her house group and felt as though she had run out of options. After the fifth break-in, she decided to contact her neighbours to see if they were having similar experiences, and if they wanted to do something about it. Their response to her inquiry was overwhelming. Around sixty households in the surrounding street said they would like to be part of a Neighbourhood Watch scheme.

Out of what was a highly disturbing experience for her, Angela and her church were able to build quality relationships with her neighbours. She did not seek to be a saint with all the answers, simply a person with similar questions to her neighbours. Angela found a practical way of addressing the problem and through her response, the streets in question have seen a significant drop in car crime.

A Neighbourhood Watch scheme may not seem much like a first-step activity, but the local church can initiate it and help to recruit more members. Even if it does not continue to be a church or home-group activity, individuals can remain in the scheme and build relationships with their neighbours.

It provides a focus for prayer

A variation on the Neighbourhood Watch scheme is what some have called the 'Neighbourhood Prayer Watch'. Churches send out letters to the surrounding neighbourhood and ask residents if they have things they would like prayer for. A specific day and time are given for the requests, which cover a broad range of issues, to be collected. Often people are prayed with there and then. A church in Bristol reported how a number of people were eagerly awaiting their arrival, and that these first contacts helped to build quality relationships.

Christians in a suburb of Nottingham have taken this idea a step further. Concerned about the amount of youth crime in the area, and the general lack of facilities for the youth, people from the churches started offering pizzas, a place for the kids to hang out, and backed up the initiative with prayer. The local police noticed a drop in crime figures on the night the church gave out pizza and asked the churches if they would like to explore a partnership. Nineteen churches in that area now pray regularly for specific issues given to them by the police. Car and property crime has dropped dramatically and is now zero on one of the most notorious streets!

This has also led to the churches being called upon to provide an 'appropriate adult' for interviews where a young person is arrested but has no available parent or guardian.

A chance to learn and grow

Neighbourhood impact is a worthy goal and as we've shown there are many things we can do to achieve it. However, instant impact is not always guaranteed and there is likely to be a steep learning curve. When the Hoole church began their fun days they were not entirely successful. They realized that they needed other activities and points of contact throughout the year if the relationships they made were to be sustainable. Initially they gained more in terms of learning from the event than the neighbourhood gained in terms of their service. In Acts chapter 6 the fledgling church was seeking to have an impact on its neighbourhood through the daily distribution of food. However, some people were being overlooked and had to complain before the church got it right.

Read together Isaiah 58:6–14 and Proverbs 21:21. See how many different 'blessings' come to those who share in some way by responding actively to the needs of those around them. Consider why this might be the case. Does anyone in the group have any examples to share from his or her own life?

These are just a few examples of ways in which relatively small initiatives can have a significant impact on the local community. The stories above have some similarities: people from the churches lead them and they do not form a part of the 'regular' church programme. Each, however, has the vital backing of the local church. The key thing is that they all seek to build relationships with people within their reach.

The Bible talks about this type of neighbourly action in Luke chapter 10. It is the story of the good Samaritan, in which an expert in Jewish law asks Jesus, 'And who is my neighbour?' (verse 29).

Having told his story, Jesus appears to be saying that anybody in need is 'my neighbour'. Taken at face value this presents the individual with a huge undertaking. How can I possibly help everyone in need? The very thought is too overwhelming to contemplate. If we look more closely at the story, however, we see similarities emerge in the circumstances of all three potential helpers:

A priest happened to be going down the same road … (verse 31)

a Levite … came to the place and saw him … (verse 32)

a Samaritan, as he travelled, came where the man was … (verse 33)

Each person mentioned above came *within reach* of the man who had been robbed and beaten, and each had the *means* to help him. Remember that 'means' refers to far more than mere finance, but includes our skills, time spent with people, our prayers, and listening to God for creative approaches to meeting community needs. The answer therefore to the question 'Who is my neighbour?' is surely that 'my neighbour' is anyone within my reach whom I have the means to help. This has far-reaching implications for today's society, which has become a 'global village' through information technology and globalization. For us, responding to those in need within our reach – while still challenging – is far more achievable than in Jesus' day.

Discuss this point within your group. Who do you feel is within your reach? Answer as individuals and reach a conclusion as a group. If you considered this before when looking at Chapter Two, now would be a good opportunity to review how you are getting on with reaching out to your 'neighbours'.

Scriptures such as the parable of the good Samaritan, which are meant to give us understanding, can sometimes make us feel inadequate. How many times have the words 'Go and do likewise' left you with a sinking feeling? We get caught in a kind of 'guilt–powerlessness cycle' that is hard to break. We feel guilty because we know we should be doing more, and then overwhelmed by the implications of helping such a vast number of those in need. Eventually we feel disillusioned and powerless. At this point we feel guilty because we haven't actually done anything and know we should be doing *something* … I'm sure you recognize the cycle.

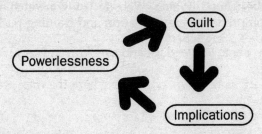

Now brainstorm some ideas as a group about what you could do that is visible, manageable, and meets real need. As you consider making some first steps, think about trying some of the ideas above, or contact REBUILD for further ideas (details at the end of the chapter).

Do's and don'ts

- Do remember that you don't have all the answers – this reduces stress, helps us to be realistic, makes us more approachable, and keeps us humble!
- Do remember that you may gain more than you give at the outset.
- Don't act out of guilt – it's a poor motivator.
- Don't act in isolation – for most things there is someone out there who can help you, and it's a good way of making connections with others.
- Don't lose hope – God is on our side, and he is with us!

Further help

REBUILD,
c/o 16 Kingston Road
London SW19 1JZ
E-mail: info@rebuild.org.uk
Website: www.rebuild.org.uk

Rebuild

Helpline: 0870 3300 213
Community weeks: 0870 3300 212

The Neighbourhood Watch Website www.nwatch.org.uk
provides comprehensive information and training packages
for new and existing schemes.

Supporting families under pressure

Nina Kelly and Eileen Jones

Families across cultural, social and economic boundaries are under pressure today as never before. Rising divorce and teenage pregnancy rates, coupled with complicated step-family relationships mean that many children don't have stable family situations or male role models in their lives.

At the same time, people's awareness of the importance of good parenting is greater than ever before. Psychology from the 1960s and 1970s has made most of today's parents aware that the quality of their parenting dramatically influences the future quality of life for their children. In addition, in an increasingly complex, uncertain and changing world, there are the pressures of bringing up children without the help of extended families.

What an opportunity for the church to shine like a light in a dark place! A wise man once said, 'Take every opportunity at all times to preach the gospel, and where necessary, use words'; and an even wiser one said, 'They shall know you are Christians by your love.'

Some inspiring stories

A group of over twenty fathers meets for breakfast once a month, not to discuss football, videos or even church business, but their role as parents. Senior business executives, naval officers and fathers on social security are re-evaluating their life goals and priorities and realizing for the first time that their families are the most important and worthwhile part of their lives. They have also begun to understand the importance of the father's role in producing tomorrow's well-adjusted confident, optimistic adults.

Andy, an information technology consultant, facilitates the men's discussions by using material which includes tips for stepdads and weekend dads. Discussion topics have ranged from the father's role in raising compassionate and caring children in a cynical and sometimes violent world to what to do if you disagree with your partner's parenting method.

The group started over a year ago, initially as a one-off parenting meeting for men to mark Father's Day. Some men came along reluctantly but, once there, enjoyed it so much that they have met every month since. 'It's so unusual to get guys together talking; but they love it there and it's a safe place for dads to talk dad's stuff,' said Andy, as surprised as anyone by the response. He has also found it a great way of gathering people in: 'Some of the guys were very much on the edge of the church and were not sure about coming along, but now they are totally involved and are there every time.' A spin-off is that many of these fathers are now interested in doing an Alpha course in the church.

These informal parenting groups are just as relevant for women, and are often welcomed by people who want to make friends and talk about issues such as parenting, that affect their everyday lives. They are also effective bridge builders for those who have just started on Alpha courses or at church.

A couple with an autistic son were inspired to reach out to other parents in the community who have children diagnosed as having autism. Nine years ago, eighteen-month-old Matthew turned from being a happy, healthy toddler, into a disruptive, uncommunicative little boy, dramatically changing life for his parents Sharon and Stephen and sister Rebecca. Guilt, well-intentioned advice, exhaustion and confusion followed before Matthew was diagnosed four-and-a-half years later with 'Semantic Pragmatic Autism'. Much of the journey since then has been rocky: they have lost and refound their Christian faith, and their mental health and marriage has suffered. But they are now emerging as stronger and more sympathetic individuals and have started a support group, 'GRASP', to help other parents with autistic children who need support, friendship and even information.

'You don't foresee having a child with special needs,' said Sharon. 'We used to look ahead thinking that ultimately it will be back to just us two; but now Matthew will be in the equation all the time and we had to adjust to that.' There are many other adjustments that parents of children with special needs have to make and that's why a support group that can offer practical, emotional and spiritual help is so vital. Stephen and Sharon had stopped going to church three years ago, when Matthew was seven, as they felt unable to take him to meetings. But through their support group, Sharon and Stephen, much to their relief, have been put in touch with churches who can welcome and accommodate Matthew.

Winchester Family Church, over the last three years, have taken the challenge of being more outward looking by reaching out to their local community in practical ways. Their basic philosophy is that churches have to be relevant to society and show by their deeds that the gospel works, that people are initially unlikely to come up to Christians and say, 'Please give me the gospel.' People will be interested, however, in the upbringing of their children and in values that touch their lives on a foundational level.

The church's main focus of activity is a 'neighbours project'. In conjunction with local health visitors and social services, church members give up a morning or afternoon each week to visit families in need. Sometimes only short-term help, a listening ear and friendship is needed. However, the volunteers do meet recurring parenting problems. Often women don't have extended family around them, live isolated lives and sometimes haven't had positive parenting role models themselves. The volunteers encourage these women to go on a 'parenting course', which the church runs four times a year.

Following on from their 'neighbours' and 'parenting' projects, the church is planning a drop-in centre, which will include monthly talks particularly with teenage single mums in mind, on topics from how to eat well on a budget, to general cookery, budgeting and childcare. The centre will include a child-friendly, non-profit-making, coffee shop.

These three stories all demonstrate how people in the community, right across social and cultural divides, can have a window into the lives of Christians and receive something of God's love and values. The stories also show how communities can be impacted by just a few people doing what is on their hearts to do.

The results of a family study published in the British Medical Journal said, 'Parenting is probably the most important public health issue facing our society. It is the single largest variable implicated in childhood illnesses and accidents, teenage pregnancy and substance misuse, truancy, school disruption and under achievement, child abuse, unemployability, juvenile crime and mental illness.' Parenting is therefore arguably one of the most important jobs in shaping the future of our world. For Christians who want their faith to be both relevant and life changing, getting involved in a parenting support group or course or a neighbours project has got to be a great way of doing that.

Discussion questions

- Read Isaiah 61:1-3. In what ways can parents be broken-hearted and captive? Reflect together on the feelings such circumstances can create. How should Christians respond, and are there any particular attitudes that should be avoided? In what practical ways can help be given by a group such as yours?

- Read Psalm 68:4-6 and James 1:27. In our society where many women are single parents and children are growing up fatherless, how can we support women without husbands and their children? Be practical. What sensitivities might we need to be careful about?

- Read John 14:6–11. The Father heart of God is at the centre of the gospel. How important is it that people in the world can see and understand this through the attitudes of Christian parents and youth workers? How can Christians inspire other parents to be good role models to their children in a world where many may have poor experiences of parenting themselves?

Do's and don'ts

- Do regularly meet new people, for example join a sports club, art class or walk anywhere you can chat to neighbours on the way. Find ways to get out and meet people.
- Do make genuine friendships with non-church people. Ask them into your home for coffee, lunch, barbecues, Christmas drinks, or whatever. Show them you are human too.
- Do make it easy for people to ask you about your Christian faith when they are ready to, without giving them a ten-point sermon.
- Do make sure that parenting groups are a mixture of church and non-church parents so that they can make friends with each other. One-third church to two-thirds non-church is best.
- Do make sure that there are other easy bridges into church life such as Alpha courses, toddler groups, and so on.
- Do use recognized, well-known parenting material as it makes working with health professionals much easier.
- Do remember when planning activities that stay-at-home mums don't have a lot of spare money.
- Do have a suitable venue with a well-organized crèche facility if planning a parenting course – not so important for ongoing informal parenting or support groups.
- Do make friends with your health visitors. Many health visitors are overworked through trying to support increasing numbers of families under pressure.

- Do get young church mums motivated to talk to other mums through school, and so on, and don't be afraid to advertise parenting groups at the school gates or at toddler groups.
- Don't say that your way of parenting is the proper way to do it.
- Don't assume all families are the same.
- Don't forget that people from different ethnic backgrounds will possess distinctive cultural understandings of what family life should be like.
- Don't patronize people treating them as if they are failures.
- Don't use your support activities to push the gospel or church on to people.

Further help

Positive Parenting
First Floor
2A South Street
Gosport, PO12 1ES
Tel: 023 9252 8787
E-mail: info@parenting.org.uk
Website: www.parenting.org.uk

For further information or resources, parenting course material or support for parents with special needs children:

Care for the Family
PO Box 488
Cardiff CF1 1RE
Tel: 029 2081 0800
E-mail: care.for.the.family@dial.pipex.com
Website: www.care-for-the-family.org.uk

For a range of resources, session material and conferences geared towards supporting family life:

The Children's Society
Edward Rudolf House
69 Margery Street
London WC1X 0JL
Tel: 020 7841 4400
Website: the-childrens-society.org.uk

The following run a wide range of children's and family projects, provide resources and publications:

Spurgeon's Child Care
74 Wellingborough Road
Rushden NN10 9TY
Tel: 01933 412 412
E-mail: scc@spurgeons.org
Website: www.garrick.co.uk/spurgeon.html

Christian Action Research and Education (CARE)
Caring Services
Challenge House
29 Canal Street
Glasgow G4 0AD
Tel: 0141 332 7212

Church Pastoral Aid Society (CPAS)
Athena Drive
Tachbrook Park
Warwick CV34 6NG
Tel: 01926 458 458
E-mail: info@cpas.org.uk
Website: www.cpas.org.uk

Family Matters
The Park
Moggerhanger
Bedford ML44 3RW
Tel: 01767 641 002
E-mail: family@familymatters.org.uk
Website: www.familymatters.org.uk

National Childbirth Trust (NCT)
Alexandra House
Oldham Terrace
London W3 6NH
Tel: 020 8992 8637

Pre-School Learning Alliance
69 King's Cross Road
London WC1X 9LL
Tel: 020 7883 0991 / 020 7883 5513 (parents' helpline)

Money worries

Keith Tondeur

One of the best ways of reaching out into your community is by helping those with financial difficulties. The reason for this is twofold. Firstly, the need is enormous. There are indications that some form of credit restriction is imposed upon one in five adults in this country. Over the past twenty years the amount of money owing on credit and store cards has increased from £4 billion to nearly £80 billion. Surveys indicate that couples argue more about money than anything else and, according to Relate, the marriage guidance agency, money worries are the major cause of relationship breakdown in over 70% of cases dealt with by the agency.

Secondly, there is a wealth of teaching in the Bible about handling money sensibly. Indeed, it has been estimated that compared to about 500 verses on prayer and on faith, there are over 2,350 on handling money. Sermons on money are not usually preached in the same ratio! By bringing the two – money problems and what the Bible teaches about money – together we can reach out into our community where so many are really hurting, bringing practical hope and often eternal hope as well We can send out a message that we care and when we do, people will ask why – and we can tell them!

Bringing hope: a story of today

Not long ago I was asked to speak about debt for a week-long series on morning television. We had several thousand calls to our helpline that day, and one woman I spoke to was in deep distress. She told me that her husband had had a breakdown; they owed over £20,000, and were thinking of declaring themselves bankrupt. I mentioned to her that the danger with bankruptcy was that if she inherited any money it might go to creditors rather than to her. She replied by saying that there was no chance of that, even though her father was wealthy, as he had refused to speak to her for seventeen years – since the day she had got married. With her permission, I rang her father up, told him what I was doing on television and of his daughter's plight.

Thirty-six hours later my phone rang and as I picked it up a voice said, 'I want to thank you for reconciling me with my daughter. I have today sent a cheque to clear her debts and this weekend I am seeing a granddaughter I didn't know I had.' He then asked why we did what we did and I explained that we were a Christian charity and simply wanted to reach out and help people in need. At the end of the conversation he made a commitment to Christ.

In today's society we need to show Jesus' love in action, putting people made in his image ahead of our own needs. Opportunities to speak about him will then inevitably arise.

What does the Bible say?

- Why do you think the Bible says, 'The borrower is the slave of the lender' (Proverbs 22:7), and 'You were bought at a price; do not become slaves of men' (1 Corinthians 7:23)?

- Romans 13:8 also says, 'Let no debt remain outstanding.' Given the above, discuss what it must feel like to be in debt.

- It would also be good to talk about the pressure put on us through advertising, mail shots, and so on, to 'buy now and pay later'. How easy it is to be seduced by such offers even if we know we cannot really afford to repay them – especially if we are struggling to make ends meet.

- Look at James 4:13, 'Now listen, you who say, "Today or tomorrow we will go to this or that city, spend a year there, carry on business and make money." Why, you do not even know what will happen tomorrow.' With very few jobs for life about, what risks are people taking on when they borrow extensively with the assumption that they will be able to repay out of future income?

The damage debt can do

We saw earlier in this chapter the damage debt can do to families. Unlike many other things it also continually gets worse if nothing is done about it because of accruing interest, often at rates of 30% or more. This constant pressure can make rational people do irrational things. It can also cause an enormous amount of stress, leading to time off work (thus often making the debt situation worse) and illness. Because one partner often does not tell the other about the full extent of the problem it usually leads to breakdown of trust and low self-esteem. People can become lonely, sometimes even cutting themselves off from friends because they can't afford their round of drinks at the pub. Sadly, if help is not available it can even lead to people taking their own lives.

What can be done?

There is much a church, or even a small group, can do to help those in their community. You might even start with your church noticeboard, seen by people every day as they walk past. What message does it relay to them? Why not show that you care by putting Credit Action's Freephone helpline number on it, as well as details of the nearest Citizens' Advice Bureau, Relate and Samaritans numbers, and so on. You can send out a message to your community that you care, and it costs you nothing. If your church has its own counsellors that too should be highlighted.

Credit Action has free posters, helpline cards, and 'Better Money Management' booklets aimed at different groups in society. As well as putting them in the church think constructively of all the places in your community that you can put them, such as libraries, social security offices, and so on. Perhaps the best place is in doctors' waiting rooms, because doctors see large numbers of people with stress-related ailments caused by money worries. We know of one surgery that gave away over three hundred copies in a year. In addition, these books also show how to do basic budgeting and it is the failure to know how to do this that is often the main reason why so many get into debt in the first place.

If, after discussion you believe that you would like to provide some form of debt counselling in your community, the first step is to raise greater awareness in the church. Organizations like Credit Action can come both to teach about and provide basic training. This is useful as not only does it encourage more people to become counsellors, it also encourages those who would like to support financially or through prayer. Importantly too, it will also give hope to those who are in debt in your church. Sadly, all figures indicate that this will be about the same percentage as in the rest of your community.

What about setting up a course on basic money management? This could include people from church and the wider community. Once you have got the course well established you can consider testing it on the young people the church has contact with, followed by offering it to local schools. Use material that has been developed by specialist organizations such as that produced by Credit Action in conjunction with Family Matters. You don't have to be a financial expert to use such materials.

Do some research in your area. Do you have a relatively

high number of students, young people or single parents? One of the easiest ways of finding out is to check the information held at the library or town hall on the last census that was done. They may well have detailed figures. Are there any colleges near you? If so, there are bound to be students there with money worries. You can think about getting in touch with the student unions to offer to run a money-management course or at least make available various leaflets and guides.

It might also be worth exploring setting up a credit union. This can take some time and requires a common bond (which can be as simple as all those who live in a particular area) before it can be established. Generally speaking, they are an effective way of lending money, as interest rates tend to be lower than anywhere else. They can be helpful to the poorer members of your communities who might otherwise have to borrow from high-interest sources or even from loan sharks. Details of how to find out about credit unions can be found at the end of this chapter. If this is too big a project for you, you can still set up a hardship fund to help meet real emergencies that you become aware of, or establish a community larder.

Other money-saving ideas which will help with overall budgeting include things like establishing community allotments by utilizing gardens people don't want or aren't able to maintain. Food co-operatives or some form of bulk-buying systems can save a lot of money. Sharing transport to the shops or providing lifts for those who would have to pay for public transport or taxis is a simple but practical way of helping, especially for those in more rural areas or on outer urban estates.

It is important that before rushing into anything, you establish what is already happening in your community. Then decide whether you want to join in making that programme more effective, or whether you want to reach out in a new area where you perceive gaps of need. Whatever you do, you'll have to get a clear feel of the make-up of your community. Nothing beats getting to know people and giving them time.

Do's and don'ts

- Do remember that money and debt are sensitive subjects. Debt books put in shops may not sell, but others put where they can be taken easily will probably vanish quickly!
- Do remember that many in debt will not have told anyone else, including their partners. So keep any knowledge you may gain strictly confidential.
- Do be creative. The more widely you distribute books, posters, and so on, the more people will be helped.
- Don't on any account try to do any debt counselling before being fully trained. Counsellors need to be licensed and also to have insurance.
- Don't think this problem will go away. With the amount of debt in this country and the number of credit and store cards in issue (47 million in Britain compared to 3 million in Germany) this problem is sadly here to stay. So any projects you plan are repeatable or for the long term.

From small beginnings

In 1992, various members of Glenwood Church in Cardiff felt that their words needed to be supported by a practical demonstration of God's love and commitment. Aware that many in their area were likely to be struggling with money issues a vision grew for a debt-counselling centre.

Credit Action helped them through teaching on the issues, thus further increasing awareness, and several volunteers were then given basic money-advice training. Starting slowly, they began reaching out into their area by way of small adverts in their local free newspaper.

Over a period of time more and more referrals came by word of mouth, and as the work expanded they were able to get funding from grant-making trusts to help them deal with the increased workload. They soon had to move out of church premises into their own offices in one of the busiest parts of Cardiff.

And so, eight years later, what had started as a small local project had grown into meeting the needs of many with money difficulties in Cardiff and its surrounding area.

Further help

Credit Action has a wide range of materials (posters, guides and courses suitable for all audiences), a Freephone debt helpline (0800 591 084), and can provide speakers for church or secular settings:

Credit Action
6 Regent Terrace
Cambridge CB2 1AA
Tel: 01223 324 034
E-mail: credit.action@dial.pipex.com
Website: www.credit.action.com

For more information on setting up a credit union:

Association of British Credit Unions
Hollyoak House
Hanover Street
Manchester M60 0AS
Tel: 0161 832 3694

Caring for the carers

Julia Burton-Jones

Who are the 'carers'?

Many people in churches care. In fact, you could even say that churches exist to care. Certainly caring is part of the role of church leaders and pastoral workers.

In the last twenty years or so, however, a new category of 'carers' has been recognized in our society. They are people who look after relatives, friends or neighbours who have a physical or mental disability, or who are frail through old age and unable to cope alone. Without the efforts of these carers, the welfare state would collapse!

Of the 5.7 million carers in Great Britain, 3.3 million are women and 2.4 million are men. In fact, 24% of people aged 45–64 are carers. Nine out of ten carers look after someone related to them. They may care for a spouse, parent, son, daughter, sibling, friend or neighbour. The person may live with the carer, or in his or her own home, or in residential care. There are also a significant number of children caring in some way for an adult parent.

As the awareness of what carers are doing has grown, there has been an increasing sense of their needs in carrying out these roles. The Carers National Association, the national charity for carers, both supports and campaigns on behalf of carers. There are also local carers projects and centres which have developed knowledge about the needs of local carers and put them in touch with the services they need.

What do carers need?

The first thing carers need is information: information about a relative's diagnosis; information about local services to help carers; information about support groups of others in the same situation. Many carers also need practical help; the task of looking after someone with special needs can be strenuous and demanding, and particularly hard to manage for carers who are elderly themselves or have other family members for whom they are caring (their own children, for example). Because the caring, no matter how fulfilling, is relentless, spanning 24 hours of the day for many, the need for breaks is high on most carers' list of priorities.

Carers often need help with feelings and relationships affected by caring. Encouragingly, this is the kind of help churches are best able to give.

Carers often feel that the concern of everyone around them is directed only towards the person for whom they are caring. No-one seems to imagine what it must be like for the carer to face the daily struggle to cope, or consider how difficult it can be to come to terms with a new and unexpected way of life.

Many carers feel angry and frustrated about their situation, and resentful of the person they are looking after because of the restrictions placed on their lives. They then see themselves as a terrible person to be in that emotional state, and feel guilty. Carers can sense that the future is bleak and lacking in hope, that there is nothing they can do to change their situation. It is not uncommon for carers to become depressed and exhausted.

That is why for many carers a listening ear is so beneficial. People in the same situation are best placed to empathize, which is why carer support groups like the Carers Christian Fellowship are vital. But with sensitivity and understanding all Christians can develop skills in listening to carers, accepting their feelings and valuing them as individuals.

Where can carers go for help?

There are many organizations involved in supporting carers and the people for whom they care. The benefits agency is there to help with the costs of caring and to provide replacement income for those who have given up work to care. Social services departments have overall responsibility for allocating services to carers. A care manager assesses the carer's needs, alongside the needs of the person for whom they care, and arranges a package of appropriate support. This might include respite care, a placement at a day centre for the cared-for person, or the back-up of the home-care service. There may be services provided by local health professionals too, for example a district nurse.

Charities like carer support groups, carer centres, and those providing support in the home or residential and respite care facilities also fulfil an important role. Private companies offer help to people in their own homes, run nursing and residential homes for short periods of respite care or on a permanent basis when carers find they can no longer care at home. Last but not least are the informal sources of help on which many carers rely: their friends and relatives, and for some their local church.

What does the Bible say?

- Read 1 Timothy 5:4 and Matthew 25:34–36. Do you see caring for a family member as part of serving God? What are some of the practical issues and dilemmas?

- Now read Galatians 6:9. Consider the sort of weariness that carers might experience. How might you encourage carers in your community and help them to see how much God values their caring?

- Read Galatians 6:2. Many carers are carrying a heavy load because they feel they have a responsibility towards a friend or family member. Are you aware of

particular needs around you? Remember the importance of safeguarding people's dignity if you are talking
about them. Are there practical ways in which you can
support people in your neighbourhood who live with
these pressures?

Ways of helping carers

Helping carers need not be time-consuming or challenging.
Small offers of help, or taking the time to spend fifteen
minutes listening to a carer, can make the world of
difference.

- *Exploring needs.* The first thing to do before offering
  help is to find out what local carers need. Carers have
  different needs according to where they live; this may
  be to do with gaps in local services, or the type of area
  in which they live, or their cultural background. Talk to
  carers you know. Contact local charities working with
  carers (you should be able to find them by contacting
  your local Council for Voluntary Service).

- *Guiding carers to sources of help.* Lots of carers find it
  hard to accept that they are 'carers'. They see themselves as simply a 'spouse', 'child', 'parent' or 'friend'
  of the person who needs them. Showing carers that
  they belong to a wider group supported by local and
  national organizations is important, as is pointing them
  in the direction of sources of help. If a carer is not
  receiving enough help, sensitively inform that they are
  entitled to a 'carers assessment' by their local social
  services department, when the needs of the person
  for whom they are caring are assessed. The Carers
  National Association helpline number (see end of
  chapter), or information about local projects publicized
  by the church, can be given to carers.

- *Working with local carers charities.* Local carer support
  organizations have contact with the carers you wish to

help and tend to know where the gaps are in what is available to carers locally. Stay in touch with them. Perhaps you can volunteer a few regular hours to work with them.

- *Offering 'befrienders'/'sitters'*. It can be difficult for carers to pop out to the shops or hairdressers, and yet even an hour to themselves can make such a difference for carers. Some churches have volunteers who befriend the cared-for person so that in time the carer feels confident enough to leave a relative for a while. Volunteers need to be prepared to learn about the person's needs from the carer.

- *Arranging a social event*. Caring can be isolating, with many carers becoming virtually 'housebound' themselves. Even if they have an opportunity for a break they may have lost touch with friends. Churches in some parts of the country provide occasional coffee mornings or lunches for carers, often arranging a parallel event for the cared-for person. This can be an opportunity to 'pamper' carers a little; some groups even call such an occasion a 'pampering day'!

- *Setting up a support group*. You might find that those who attend the social events above would like to be involved in a more regular get-together with others in a similar situation. Meeting with others who are in similar situations can be a source of support, a sense that there are people who understand.

Ideas for action

- How could you consult local carers to find out what they need?
- Which organizations in your area support carers? How could you make sure carers find out about them?
- Is there a member of the congregation who could 'network' local carers organizations?

- Are there people in your church who relieve carers by sitting with the person for whom they are caring for an hour or two? Could this service be offered more widely?
- How about inviting local carers to a coffee morning, meal or party as a way of thanking them for the vital role they fulfil in your community? Is there a local carers support group you could link up with in offering this?
- Have you asked carers whether they would like to be involved in the setting up of a support group if a local one doesn't already exist?

Golden rules for supporting carers

Members of the Carers Fellowship were recently invited to put forward ideas for churches wanting to offer more support to carers. Here are some of their comments:

I appreciated what members of my church did for me when I was caring at home: invitations to lunch; sitting for a couple of hours so I could go out; a couple of people I could always ring if I got desperate ...

My golden rule for supporting carers is to listen, without interruption, to the carer's outpourings. I would like to see churches offering carers friendship, support (the kind that is requested) and practical help on a regular basis. To offer advice without being asked can be very frustrating to a carer who has in all probability exhausted most channels open to them.

Don't offer the carer what you think is *good for them*. In asking what help the carer wants, list a few suggestions, such as a book from the library or company for an hour at the carer's chosen time, or a home-made cake.

Be a good listener, be a regular prayer, and always ask after the carer as well as the patient.

Encourage carers in their role. Offer to take the person being cared for out.

Do's and don'ts

The list below summarizes the views of the members of the Carers Christian Fellowship:

- Do be prepared to spend time listening to carers.
- Do ask after the carer, not just the person they care for.
- Do be sensitive in quoting Bible verses, offering spiritual encouragement gently.
- Do be specific in offering help, giving an idea of what you can offer.
- Do be patient, as it may take carers a while to place trust in you.
- Do be reliable, confident you can fulfil your promise before offering help.
- Don't give advice, however tempting it may be to come up with 'solutions'.
- Don't be judgmental, but accept carers with all their mixed-up feelings.

In 1995 the Diocese of Blackburn received 'Opportunities for Volunteering' funding to set up Share and Care. Paid coordinators recruit, train and support volunteers recruited from local churches to befriend elderly people, accompany them on shopping or other outings, and support carers. Referrals come from a variety of sources such as the social services, doctors and health visitors. The idea behind Share and Care is to extend the caring work of the church into the wider community. Share and Care has grown to be a truly ecumenical organization which operates over most of the Fylde coast and Lancaster.

Marjorie is a carer who lives near Blackpool. Her frail elderly father lives next door. One of the difficulties she encountered was anxiety over going away on holiday. She asked Share and Care to provide a volunteer who would visit her dad while she was away. Emily, the volunteer from the local Methodist church, struck up a friendship with Marjorie's father. He began to look forward to her visits and appreciated her respect and interest as he recounted stories from his younger life. Even when he was feeling low, Emily managed to bring a twinkle to his eye. When Marjorie was away for a couple of weeks taking a much-needed break, she was able to relax in the knowledge that Emily was keeping an eye on her father.

Syon Mission Church, Brentford, a church associated with the national social action organization, the Shaftesbury Society, has for several years hosted a regular but informal gathering of local carers. They meet each week in the church lounge area to chat, drink coffee and just be with each other. They all have adult children with learning disabilities and these carers share common concerns about their future capacity as they get older to be the main carer.

Further help

The Carers Christian Fellowship offers support from a Christian perspective to people caring for relatives and friends, and links churches with local members for advice over plans for helping carers:

Sue Jones
Coordinator
Carers Christian Fellowship
14 Cavie Close
Nine Elms
Swindon SN5 5XD
Tel: 01793 887 068

A national charity for carers offering advice, publications, and campaigns on national issues:

Carers National Association
First Floor
20 Glasshouse Yard
London EC1A 4JS

Rebuild

Tel: 020 7490 8898
Fax: 020 7490 8824
Helpline: 0808 808 7777
Website: www.carersuk.demon.co.uk

A number of the member organizations of the REBUILD Coalition will offer home support or residential care services. Visit the REBUILD Website (www.rebuild.org.uk) or contact the telephone helpline (0870 3300 213) for more information.

Support for older people

Sharon Craddock

Avoiding the stereotypes

One group of people who are often identified as a particularly dependant and vulnerable group in society are those who are elderly. We are moved by compassion for those whom we see in ill health in residential and nursing homes. Their degree of vulnerability is high and this stirs within us feelings of wanting to protect and comfort. Equally, we may fear being in a similar position ourselves one day.

There is a general view in society that older people are sick, confused, complaining and lonely. In fact, most older people live in their own homes and many are in good health, and have life experience and skills to offer. Some live in sheltered accommodation (and may receive services such as home help), while others live with or are supported by family members. Therefore, in supporting older people within the community it is important to recognize that the elderly population is diverse. Consequently there are a range of responses that can be made by those wanting to get involved.

Loss

For many older people the experience of loss is a day-to-day reality. The concept of 'loss' can be applied to many situations which can affect each of us as we grow older. Physical deterioration and disabilities can result in the loss of control of one's own body, and restricted mobility can result in losing the ability to visit relatives and friends, and even travelling for short distances can become impossible. Other losses can include the death of friends and relatives: older people can suffer frequent bereavements. A reduced ability to remember things, or to solve problems effectively, can be keenly experienced as loss. It is during these times that meaningful relationships are important. Relationships that give a sense of being valued, communicate respect and love.

What does the Bible say?

- Read Leviticus 19:32; Proverbs 16:31; 20:29; and Job 12:12. What do these verses teach us about how older people are to be regarded? Contrast these with contemporary attitudes. Consider what the role of Christians is and what we can do to present a challenge to the prevailing negative attitudes in society.

- Now look at Romans 12:4, 5. What are some of the possible implications for the way in which older people are involved in your church? Explore together what wider application you think the principles in these verses could have in your local community.

- Now think about what you have read so far in this chapter. On a piece of paper write down one thing that you have learnt or been reminded of, and then something that you are going to do differently as a result. It could be about a change of attitude or a concrete action. Share these with others in the group, and pray for each other.

Where do I fit in?

It can be quite daunting to consider the diverse needs of the many older people in the community and how to help to fulfil these needs. Questions may include the following: Do I have enough experience or the necessary skills? What knowledge do I have to support this individual appropriately? Do I have the time? Can I stick with this person or will I get overwhelmed? What do I do if …? These questions may be fuelled by fear of taking risks or lack of confidence. We must be realistic about our limitations, and not promise things we can't deliver.

Remember, if we are unable to offer practical support we can offer emotional and spiritual support. For example each of us has within our grasp the ability to offer kindness, to share our hopes and aspirations and, indeed, our friendship.

It is wonderful to have a vision and a cause that different members of a church can contribute towards achieving. Don't fall into the trap, however, of thinking you're the only answer! Older people need to be treated with the dignity that is rightfully theirs, and they should have a say about what assistance they would find of benefit.

Although the process of identifying needs and the challenges that are faced can be 'exciting', putting these ideas into action is generally where most people fall down. The first rule of putting our words into action is to develop a plan or strategy for the group. Suggestions of key areas to include in that 'strategy' are as follows.

Ideas for action

Discover the needs of the older people in your community

- Find out where older people live.
- Find and locate the names of local residential and nursing homes.
- Consult your church leader for the names of older people in your congregation who are unable to attend church or who are housebound.

- Consult older people themselves about what the church could usefully do in the community to support them (for example by using a short questionnaire, and also talking to those with whom you are already in contact). Ask them what they would like to do and how the church could help facilitate it.

Find out about other organizations

- Find out what other churches are doing in the community.
- Consult the local social services and district nurses about needs in your area and the sort of help your group is thinking about developing.
- Find out what local charitable organizations there are that can offer help and advice (like Age Concern, or Help the Aged, the Red Cross or the Women's Royal Voluntary Service).
- Are there local day centres or residential homes that are looking for voluntary befrienders?

Next steps

- Share your views, ideas and aspirations with others in your group.
- Compare these with what you have found out about needs in the community (and your church) among older people.
- Identify what support – practical, emotional and spiritual – you can provide to older church members and the wider community.
- Decide what the next steps are and how you are going to support one another (for example you could meet to share your experiences and pray).
- Decide on a point of reference for everyone (for example your home-group leader).

Practical and social support

It is important to be realistic about what help and support we can provide. Below are some examples of activities that can support older people in the community:

- starting a befriending scheme
- helping those at home with shopping and household tasks
- creating opportunities for older people to meet with others
- enabling an older person in some way to become a valued member of your extended family, where they can give as well as receive
- invitations and transport to church events and activities
- holding coffee mornings and hospitality events, but making sure that the older people get a chance to be involved – not everything being done to them and for them
- offering to sit with someone while their carer has a break
- visiting, telephoning or sending a card
- finding out about respite care or finding someone who can advise
- doing voluntary work with an established organization

Emotional and spiritual support

- listening
- sharing
- reminiscing and finding meaning in history and lessons learnt
- being a sounding board for anger and frustration
- acknowledging fears about the future
- sharing aspirations for the future, and taking them seriously
- crying and laughing together
- taking part in services in homes
- spending times of prayer, reading Bible passages and psalms to individuals
- remembering older people you know when you pray

What does the individual need to think about?

In preparing to support older people it is important that those within the church are honest with themselves and each other. Helping others can bring great satisfaction but it also has its costs. These include time, emotions and commitment to persevere. For example as trust develops, emotions of anger and delight can be shared and feelings can be hurt. It is also important to remember that when entering someone's home we are a guest and a non-judgmental attitude is required.

Listed below are suggested areas on which the individual needs to reflect prior to beginning to support older people.

Carers' emotional toolkit

- commitment
- honesty with ourselves and others
- openness
- non-judgmental attitude towards others
- awareness of cost of time and emotions
- dependence upon God for wisdom

And remember ...

It is also important to remember that we should not be deterred by or become upset by someone who does not want to share and spend any more time with visitors. We have to respect that choice but still make sure to pray for them. We all change day to day and there may be another time when contact can be made, so determination and perseverance are perhaps two other tools we can add, if needed, to our toolkit. Gradually with experience comes the knowledge of knowing the timing and length of visits and how the type of support should progress.

The benefits from sharing relationships with older people include learning from their wealth of experience, their wisdom and the passing on of their lives and histories. Even those who are unable to communicate verbally can offer love and affirm those who care for them. This can lead to a sense of meaning in our work, which in itself can bring satisfaction and enjoyment.

Good neighbours

A church in a rural village in North Nottingham were willing to be involved in their local community but were struggling to identify any gaps in what was already being provided. Then a development officer from the Council for Voluntary Service researched the village, looking particularly at the needs of older people and the services that were then on offer. The need for a Good Neighbours scheme was identified and the development officer approached the local minister to talk about the possibility. (The minister was out so they spoke to his wife instead!) Subsequently they set the project up.

Members of the church are involved alongside other members of the community, and the minister's wife acts as the coordinator for fifty-five volunteers. 'Ravenshead Ready Call' offers help with transport, shopping, collecting prescriptions, occasional gardening, and so on. Although the publicity does not specify age, most of the people using the scheme are elderly.

On the basis of involvement with the Good Neighbours scheme other things have evolved as friendships have developed and further needs have been identified. Once a month church members use the community minibus to take a group of older people out for an early evening meal; three times a year the church lays on a cooked Sunday lunch; and once a month a lunch group meets in a local school. The church are now involved in discussions about setting up a day centre.

Out of the work done in the community the church's image has completely changed. Molly Bell, minister's wife and coordinator of Good Neighbours scheme said, 'They have seen us now; they know who we are and that we do what we say we will do. Our desire to be "Ashwood, the church in the community" has become a reality.'

Further help

Trinity Care plc
15 Musters Road
West Bridgford
Nottingham NG2 7PP
Tel: 0115 945 5485
Fax: 0115 982 1919
E-mail: enquiry@trinitycare.co.uk

Methodist Homes for the Aged
Epworth House
Stuart Street
Derby DE1 2EQ
Tel: 01332 296 200
Fax: 01332 296 925

Shaftesbury Housing Association
Shaftesbury House
87 East Street
Epsom KT17 1DT
Tel: 01372 727 252
Fax: 01372 736 800
Website: www.shaftesburyhousing.org.uk

Age Concern England
Astral House
1268 London road
London SW16 4ER
Tel: 020 8679 8000
E-mail: infordep@ace.org.uk
Website: www.ace.org.uk

Help the Aged
St James Walk
Clerkenwell Green
London EC1R 0BE
Tel: 020 7253 0253
E-mail: infor@helptheaged.org.uk

Website: www.helptheaged.org.uk

Carers National Association
First Floor
20 Glasshouse Yard
London EC1A 4JS
Tel: 020 7490 8898
Fax: 020 7490 8824
Carers Line: 0808 808 7777
Website: www.carersuk.demon.co.uk

People with disabilities

Paul Dicken

Setting the scene

The World Health Organization states that there are over 650 million people with disabilities in the world. If they were gathered together to form one nation, that nation would be the world's third largest country, after China and India. As a nation (and as a people group in every society) they would

- be the poorest in the world;
- be the least educated;
- have the least access to any sort of transport;
- be the lowest proportion in employment;
- be the least evangelized and have the lowest proportion with church involvement.

In the UK there are about 9 million disabled people or elderly people who are disabled by the effects of the ageing process. If you add to that figure a similar number of carers, you get a truer picture of the number of people affected by disability. After all, if a building is inaccessible to, say, a wheelchair user, then it will be inaccessible to that person's husband, wife or children.

In Luke 14:21, 23 Jesus instructed us to 'Go out quickly into the streets and alleys of the town and bring in the poor, the crippled, the blind and the lame ... Go out to the roads and country lanes and make them come in, so that my house will be full.' In reality, we see relatively few people with disabilities in our churches. Many disabled Christians come to faith because someone was prepared to make a little extra effort and spend a little more time to make sure that they could be included in activities and events. Anything you do should be done with the attitude that the body of Christ is incomplete without disabled people: 'those parts of the body that seem to be weaker are indispensable' (1 Corinthians 12:22). We need to be inclusive not to 'look after' disabled people, but to ensure that we benefit from their presence with us and that they have the opportunity to know Christ's love.

One person's contribution

So often disabled people feel and, indeed, are undervalued. Mary has had both legs amputated; she has diabetes, angina and cerebral palsy. She was keen to help with one of the church's youth groups, so the leaders arranged that the youngsters should meet in her home, which worked well for her as it was wheelchair-friendly. The children saw disability in a new way and all the care staff who called at other times asked Mary about the children's work which was put up on her walls. This gave Mary an opportunity to share her faith.

On another occasion Mary took over the ironing for a household of five people where a couple were nursing the husband's elderly mother. It probably took Mary three times longer than a non-disabled person would have taken, but the family could not have managed without Mary for the six months she did that service. She felt (and was) needed and valued. Think about how you can draw in disabled people as a church resource.

How can you make a difference in the lives of disabled people in your area? It's important to start from the place that people with disabilities are people first, precious to God, people for whom Christ died. They may use wheelchairs, see through their guide dog's eyes, or even speak by using their hands. However, God sees them in exactly the same way he sees a non-disabled person, as precious and important. You don't have to be an expert to reach out to a disabled person; they will tell you what to do if they need any sort of assistance.

It is important to look at our attitudes and to make sure that we have the right motivation.

What does the Bible say?

- What should our motive be to reach out to disabled people? Read 2 Samuel 9 and 2 Corinthians 5:12–14 for guidance. If we don't have the right motivation we may bring the wrong attitudes, burn out quickly, and will establish little. These passages help us understand that the motive for getting involved does not reside in our feelings towards disabled people, but in our loyalty to Christ. Notice that David did not know Mephibosheth was disabled before making a commitment. David showed kindness to him out of his loyalty to Jonathan. Working with disabled people is often viewed merely as 'helping' or 'doing for'. Unfortunately, such an approach misses two important truths. First, we are talking about two-way relationships. Second, however profound their disability, all disabled people are able to give as well as receive. We need to be very careful to deal with any patronizing attitudes we might hold inside us.

- Is it a mistake when someone is born with a disability? Read Psalm 139 and Exodus 4:11–12 for background. If it is not a mistake, why do you think someone would be born with, or experience a disability?

- In New Testament times, as now, people with disabilities, faced difficulties in daily living. Match the scriptures below to the corresponding problem on the right. And then consider what the experience of these things could feel like:

Acts 3:1–5	accessibility
John 5:7	being pushed aside
Luke 5:18–19	communication
Mark 5:26	earning a living
Mark 7:32	finances
Mark 10:46–50	health and safety
Leviticus 13:45–46	housing
Luke 14:21	lack of help
Matthew 17:14–16	social isolation

- What skills do I need? Luke 5:17–26 provides some insight for us. What special skills did the friends of the disabled man need? How did they solve the problem they met? What part did the man himself play, and what were the choices that his friends helped him make?

Ideas for action

Hold a Disability Sunday

Your home group could arrange a Disability Sunday at your church, a day when the church service focuses on disability issues from a Christian perspective. Invitations can be given out in local residential homes, schools and organizations for disabled people, emphasizing that the church wants to understand more about disability issues. The service itself can include personal stories or testimonies from disabled people in the church; a sermon focusing on the contribution every person, including disabled people, can make; and possibly sketches and songs by some disabled people. The Sunday school, Bible classes and youth meetings could all reflect the theme.

Find people in your area with disabilities

Sensitively find out who in your church has a disability, or have family members at home who have; find out where the residential, nursing and community homes are. Contact any local organizations that specialize in disability; find out what they do and what gaps they think there are in local support for people with disabilities and their families.

Then tackle the question of why the church doesn't have contact with them. The reason why they don't come to the church might be a simple issue of transport. Vehicles suitable for wheelchair users can be accessed through building links with local community transport groups. Ask individual members of your church to join a rota to collect disabled and elderly people.

However, the first place to start is by establishing a relationship, not by expecting people to come to church. Don't forget that building relationships with people with disabilities includes accepting their hospitality, and taking the initiative to visit them in their own homes. Don't expect them to do things on your terms just because they have a disability.

Improve access in your church and homes

This isn't just about wheelchairs (only 5% of disabled people are wheelchair users). Think about people with partial sight who need large print or hearing-aid users who need a loop. The organization Through The Roof has material to help you do an access audit.

Share the demands upon Christian families with disabled children

Parents of disabled children are often stretched and can find life highly stressful. Make time to listen, and in a non-judgmental way, because sometimes these parents will have strong feelings, possibly of a negative nature. Look for ways you can support the parents, such as offering to sit in church with the child during a service or in Sunday school. Invite the child to your home for a meal or a trip out and give the parents a break. See what other practical help you can give the family. Remember that certain periods, such as when their child reaches seven and they are 'statemented' by the education authorities as needing special schooling can be particularly stressful. This may feel as if their child is being labelled for life.

Do's and don'ts

Disabled people in general

- Do treat people with disabilities as you would anyone else.
- Do always speak directly to the person who has a disability.
- Do always ask the person who has a disability if you can help him or her in any way.
- Do whenever possible, seat disabled people with their friends or family.
- Do be aware that people may have hidden disabilities such as epilepsy or Alzheimer's disease, and may need help.
- Don't use negative terms such as 'crippled' or 'victim'.
- Don't consider a companion or carer to be a conversational go-between.
- Don't assume anything – always ask!

People with visual impairment

- Do identify yourself by name.
- Do show a blind person to his or her seat.
- Do ensure they know if you can provide large print or braille material.
- Do explain to a visually impaired person where things are located.
- Do provide space for a guide dog to lie by removing a chair, and agree with the person on how much fuss should be made of the dog!
- Don't push visually impaired people – always allow them to take your arm.

People with hearing impairment

- Do speak clearly and slowly.
- Do look directly at the person and speak at normal speed with clear lip patterns.

- Don't obscure your face; ensure your face and mouth can be seen clearly.
- Don't exaggerate or shout.
- Don't speak directly into the person's ear.

People with speech impairment

- Do give your whole, unhurried attention with good eye contact.
- Don't finish a sentence or word for the person.
- Don't get agitated or impatient

People with mobility difficulties

- Do always ask a wheelchair user if she or he would like assistance before you help.
- Do try to sit or kneel to talk to wheelchair users so that eye contact is easier.
- Do provide a seat near the entrance in public meeting places so that the disabled person doesn't need to move far.
- Don't push wheelchair users unless they ask you to do so.
- Don't hold on to or lean on a person's wheelchair.

People with learning disabilities

- Do be patient, give someone with learning disabilities plenty of time.
- Don't assume the person cannot understand you.

Acting it out

A group of Christians, drawn from various churches in the Harlow area of Essex started a Christian group for adults with learning disabilities (a Causeway Prospects group). The members of the group were encouraged to develop their acting skills, and now have a small repertoire of extremely moving drama sketches that they perform at conferences and events around the country. Even more exciting has been their work with homeless people on the streets. People with learning disabilities that would normally be written off as having nothing to contribute are reaching people in need in a way that others can't!

Further help

Causeway Prospects
PO Box 351
Reading RG1 7AL
Tel: 0118 950 8781
Fax: 0118 939 1683
E-mail: causeway@prospects.org.uk
Website: www.prospects.org.uk

Torch Trust for the Blind
Torch House
Hallaton
Market Harborough LE16 8UJ
Tel: 01858 555 301
Fax: 01858 555 371
E-mail: torchtrust@dial.pipex.com

Deaf Christian Network
PO Box 212
Doncaster DN2 5XA
Tel: 01302 369 684 (voice/minicom)
Fax: 01302 739 660
E-mail: deafcn@dircon.co.uk
Website: www.deafcn.dircon.co.uk

Hard of Hearing Christian Fellowship
PO Box 91
Reading RG1 5YR
Tel: 0118 987 2166
E-mail: graeme_naish@compuserve.com

Through The Roof and Disabled Christians Fellowship
PO Box 178
Cobham
Surrey KT11 1YN

Rebuild

Tel: 01932 866 333 (minicom)
Fax: 01932 866 333
E-mail: info@throughtheroof.org
Website: www.throughtheroof.org

Church Action on Disability
50 Scrutton Street
London EC2A 4PH
Tel: 020 7452 2085
Fax: 020 7452 2001

The Shaftesbury Society
Church Development Services
16 Kingston Road
London SW19 1JZ
Tel: 020 8239 5555
Website: www.shaftesburysoc.org.uk

Literacy and work

Simon Pellew and Sarah Thomas

For the person reading this chapter illiteracy is almost unimaginable. Your day is filled with reading: road signs, instructions, forms, bills, as well as newspapers, this book and the Bible. Yet for a large proportion of the population reading and writing are a serious problem, preventing them from getting a reasonable job or from helping their children with schoolwork, and making everyday life a constant struggle with the risk of embarrassing mistakes.

How serious is the problem?

Reports from the Basic Skills Agency says that between 10% and 15% of the adult population have literacy or numeracy problems. The situation is worse for people over fifty and around half of all unemployed people have literacy problems. Around 80% of people in prison have literacy difficulties.

Poor basic skills affect every aspect of a person's life, and continue to do so throughout adulthood. Such people are less likely to vote or to be members of a community organization. The literacy levels required in the workplace are rising, as employers now generally require literacy even for manual jobs because of health-and-safety regulations.

Why there are people with poor literacy and numeracy in our society:

107

- failure of schools to spot children with difficulties
- learning difficulties
- disrupted education
- lack of parental support
- immigration and poor English

But things don't have to stay this way. The real-life stories below powerfully illustrate this!

Dareb's story

Dareb was stuck at home, a single mum looking after two young children. Originally from Sierra Leone she had moved to the UK as a young woman. Family troubles meant she was effectively on her own and she was suffering from depression.

Dareb had not been to school since a young age and was unable to read and write beyond a basic level. She could just about manage to write her name but not her address. She was lacking in confidence in terms of her skills and also socially.

At Pecan, the employment training charity we work for in South-East London, we try to reach people by systematically door-knocking the large housing estates. Someone from Pecan knocked on Dareb's door. As a result she started coming to the One-to-One Literacy project held in church premises. A volunteer from a local church worked with her to make sure that the teaching was tailored to her needs. She was particularly interested in gardening and growing her own vegetables and so the tutor developed some special materials for her.

It was not easy for Dareb. She was not confident and was told by others that she shouldn't be learning to read. Her life was full of pressures. Sometimes she would arrive at the project in tears. Her tutor would talk with her, comfort her, help her and the project team would pray for her. The literacy project was probably the only stable element in her life. It was a safe place to come where people would listen, help and stick by her.

Through contact with one of the volunteers at the project Dareb started coming to church. This made a great difference in her life. She brought her children along too and began to make friends there. She joined a 'just looking' group, has made a commitment to the Lord and is soon to be baptized!

Recently she has seemed much brighter and more confident. People have noticed. Her reading and writing have improved and she has joined a small group, something she would never have had the confidence to do before. When both her children are at school she wants to get a job.

Wayne's story

Wayne is in his mid-thirties and has a wife and three children. He used to be a painter and decorator but has struggled to find employment for a while. He is anxious about his inability to read and write. As an unemployed adult he was referred to the literacy project at Pecan but it took him a year to pluck up courage to attend.

Lack of confidence is his main difficulty, as being unable to read or write is hard to admit. Wayne felt a failure; he had had a bad experience learning at school and felt he was stupid. As a result of falling behind and the teacher not seeming to have time for the 'slow ones' in class, he became disruptive and never learnt to read or write.

His children would bring books home from school and ask Dad to read them. He would make excuses. One day his daughter found his file with work from Pecan and made fun of him in front of visitors. She didn't know that he couldn't read. Wayne found this difficult to deal with.

His tutor has had to persevere with Wayne who has needed constant encouragement, and regular reminding of the things he *can* do and what he *has* achieved, rather than the things he struggles with.

However, he is gradually gaining ground. He seems to have grown in confidence and shows genuine joy as he takes tiny steps forward. He can now read books with his daughter. Through coming to the project he has realized that he is not the only one who struggles with literacy and that there is hope for him. In his words, 'I feel great about coming to Pecan; it has given me a new lease of life.'

What does the Bible say?

Although the Bible does not discuss literacy directly, there are key principles related to employment that apply to our contemporary society.

- Read Genesis 1:21–31; 2:15; 3:17–19. These verses describe how human beings were given, right from the beginning of time, responsibility for the world around them. If everyone has that responsibility by virtue of being human, what are the implications of being excluded from work opportunities because of not having the right skills?

- What clues does Deuteronomy 15:4–11 give us about what our attitudes should be to those who are poor and disadvantaged? How might this apply when thinking about the needs of people in Dareb's and Wayne's situations?

- Consider 1 Thessalonians 4:11, 12. What jobs don't require literacy? Are these 'good' jobs? What makes a 'good' job?

- A general question: Is it possible to survive in our society without the ability to read or write? How would you cope?

- And another general question: The church historically encouraged education so that people could read the Bible. Is literacy essential to be able to participate in your church's life? Would someone with poor reading or writing feel self-conscious there?

Ideas for action

For most people the greatest contribution anyone can make is to treat them with respect and care. Poor literacy damages a person's self-esteem; Christians are often pretty good at building people up through respect, encouragement and support.

There are various levels of action you can take. To help someone improve their reading and writing takes time and lots of patience. There is no point in starting if you are not prepared to work with the person for at least three months. It took most of us several years to master reading and writing with an English class several times a week, and adults have a lot more to overcome, especially if they are trying to recover from a history of failure with education and learning.

If you want to get involved (and it can be extremely rewarding) then you can

- offer to help at a local college or charity running literacy classes;
- ask your church leader if they know of anyone who needs help (this would have to be done tactfully);
- contact your local prison to see if they have a literacy programme and offer to volunteer as a listener if they do have one – there are great problems in prisons;
- prevent problems by helping with reading at a local school.

If you have some experience with adult literacy then you could consider starting a literacy class. This might be general literacy or perhaps teaching English for a purpose (for example for employment, to help your children read, writing letters, using e-mails, and so on). This might make recruiting people easier. A recently developed idea is 'family literacy' where a whole family is helped. This is important because children of parents with literacy difficulties often struggle as well.

One advantage of tutoring in literacy or numeracy is that

you can provide a useful service without much equipment or any advanced training. Ideally, you will be able to provide access to a computer, because, for many people, writing on a computer can be an encouraging experience as it allows them to produce a tidy (and spell-checked) document without it being obvious that they are poor writers. There is also some excellent software that can help people. Tutors should make sure they get some basic training.

Recruiting is always difficult because people are reluctant to risk more failure (and it is hard work trying to learn to read and write). We find recruiting for literacy is much easier than for numeracy, though, perhaps because people find numeracy more of a problem. Useful contacts can be as follows:

- *The Jobcentre*, as they will be trying to place people in work and so will be aware of their literacy levels.

- *Schools* may have pinpointed parents with difficulties. The school might be prepared to let you use their premises, especially if you were going to be developing family literacy, but they would want to be reassured that your tutors were thoroughly trained.

- *Colleges*, as they may have waiting lists. They will be reluctant to refer people to you, however, unless they are confident that you can offer a high-quality service.

Starting a project is difficult as the issues can be complex and there is a need to make sure the tutoring is of a high standard. We have found that the best way is to learn from other people's mistakes perhaps by spending time with them as a volunteer before starting on your own.

Ideas of other ways of assisting those with employment problems include the following:

- creating structured volunteering opportunities at the church or in your workplace so that people can gain useful work experience as well as something positive to go on a CV

- using under-utilized church premises as a low-cost base for someone to set up their own business
- putting them in touch with (and going with them to make enquiries if they would appreciate it) the various courses that are run by colleges to help people on the first rung of the ladder towards a job
- teaching someone basic computer skills and letting them practice on your computer
- creating a supported environment where people can follow up job adverts using a phone or e-mail facilities

Loans that change lives

Ayelach runs a small kiosk from her home in a slum in Addis Ababa, Ethiopia. It's the only source of income for her and the children, as her husband abandoned her, and her home and possessions were destroyed in a fire. She was able to set up this small business with a loan from a local church who have been running several credit and loan schemes in the slums. She is gradually repaying the money, and feels that they have helped her to make a new start in life – she now has a job and hope for the future.

Further help

The best place to get information, research and ideas is the Basic Skills Agency (www.basic-skills.co.uk). This is a Government body that commissions research and provides funding for basic skills. They also sponsor a quality standard for basic skills tuition. Most colleges provide basic skills tuition. The standard and approach can vary enormously, with some colleges keen to work with community organizations.

Pecan Ltd
1 Atwell Road
London SE15 4TW

Rebuild

Tel: 020 7740 9200
Fax: 020 7525 9201

Vines Centre Trust
Vineswood House
Gas House Road
Rochester ME1 1PN
Tel: 01634 406 245
E-mail: paul.robinson@vinescentre.org.uk

Latymer Training Centre
116–118 Bramley Road
North Kensington
London W10 6SU
Tel: 020 8968 5952
E-mail: latymer.training@shaftesburysoc.org.uk

Homelessness

Brendan Bowles

You merely have to walk through the centre of any medium-sized town to know that homelessness is a serious problem. Official statistics show that 104,700 households in the UK were dealt with as homeless in 1999. But that doesn't count the thousands of singles or childless couples who get almost no help. The figures are massive. And the impact on people affected is disastrous.

Church groups have often taken a lead in providing help. A few people decide something must be done. They plan a small project. They feel alone and ill-equipped. But they do it anyway. They help a few people, and encounter problems. They solve the problems, survive, get organized, raise funds, develop their expertise, expand the project. Sometimes their example inspires others to copy what they have done. And so small beginnings mushroom and have a major effect on a growing number of people's lives.

The three initiatives described below by various churches in Leeds demonstrate this.

Caring for life

Young people who have been abused as children often end up homeless and friendless. Their disturbed behaviour isolates them from people their own age and from normal channels of help. Some have learning difficulties and find it impossible to cope alone. Those who survive often become perpetual offenders – for many there appears to be no alternative to crime, alcohol, drugs, or even suicide.

Peter Parkinson, pastor of Leeds Reformed Baptist Church, along with members of his congregation, became aware of this local need just over ten years ago. Together they formed Caring For Life, a registered Christian charity providing practical and down-to-earth help for homeless, vulnerable young people. Caring For Life's aim is to provide homes in which young people are given consistent and sensitive long-term care – for life if necessary. Ongoing support is given to those who move into their own accommodation to make sure they are not lonely and can cope.

One of Caring For Life's first projects was Tindall House, which provides a home for eight young men for as long as they wish to stay. This lack of any time limit on the length of stay has helped most residents experience a great sense of emotional security. On average residents stay for three years, but no-one is ever made to move on. In this way Tindall House provides an ideal environment in which severely damaged young people can escape from their painful past and discover their true potential. For many of its residents, Tindall House is the first place they can really call home.

Caring For Life has developed other projects including Crag House Farm. This is fully stocked and equipped, and offers experience in agriculture, horticulture, animal husbandry, conservation, woodwork and car maintenance. Here young people can gain work experience and learn to work with others. Learning to care for animals has been identified as one of the most successful ways of reaching into the hearts and minds of the most severely damaged young people.

A home is where you belong, where you are cared for, and can be useful – it's more than a roof.

Nightstop UK

Nightstop UK meets a different need in a different way. It draws on volunteer hospitality to provide emergency accommodation for young people with nowhere else to go. How did it get started?

About fifteen years ago the famous *Faith in the City* report encouraged churches to get involved in helping poor people in urban areas. So a small group of Leeds churches met and identified a priority need: there was no emergency accommodation for young single people. But what to do?

They involved Barnardo's and Churches and Neighbourhood Action (CANA) in a brainstorming session. Between them they came up with the simple idea of providing accommodation in the homes of approved volunteers. They developed a set of ground rules for the scheme which continue to provide the framework. In effect they invented a wheel that is still spinning.

From 1987 to 1990 there was only the one scheme in Leeds, which worked well. Then in 1990 groups sprang up in Birmingham and Durham. In 1992 a BBC programme in the *Everyman* series called 'Entertaining angels' featured the scheme. Next morning there were three hundred calls from churches wanting to start a scheme.

Since then Barnardo's have overseen the development of more schemes to today's total of thirty-two, which still involve many Christians. Nightstop UK is becoming a national charity in its own right, however, with the aim of supporting existing schemes and creating seven new ones by 2002.

St George's Crypt

St George's Crypt, Leeds, is another scheme. It was born in 1930 from the vision of the Rev. Don Robins, a First World War fighter pilot. Don saw the symptoms of the Depression, unemployment, hunger, hardship and despair. In his first sermon he said, 'This must be a church wherein may be found the life of a Christian family, not as a theory, but as a living fact.'

Under the church was a crypt full of coffins, with holes in the walls and a floor covered with dust. Don covered the coffins and opened it as a day shelter with food and drink provided by the congregation.

Seventy years later there are new needs and the work has expanded considerably. At the start of the new millennium St George's Crypt is a large charity employing a team of around thirty paid staff and eighty or so volunteers. The charity aims to provide professional standards of care within a framework of Christian faith and witness to the clients, all of whom are treated with dignity and respect, regardless of age, sex, ethnic origin or religious beliefs.

These are three examples chosen at random in Leeds. But they all illustrate a particular point: start small and see how it spreads. The same principle is seen across the country where Christians have been at the heart of setting up housing associations, rent-deposit schemes, hostels, emergency accommodation, soup-runs and many other projects.

The Christian beginnings have been small. But the impact on society has been immense. As Jesus said, 'The kingdom of heaven is like yeast that ... worked all through the dough' (Matthew 13:33).

What does the Bible say?

Should we stop to help?

Read Luke 10:30–37. The Samaritan is called 'good' because he stopped to help. But were the others so awful? Here are ten reasons for not stopping. Put them in order, with the most convincing first:

- If I helped this person it might encourage others to get beaten up and robbed.
- My wife would be angry if I got blood on my clothes.
- Being seen in public with that kind of person could damage my reputation.
- I was frightened of getting involved.
- I was embarrassed to talk to a stranger.
- Stopping to help would have made me late – punctuality is a virtue.
- I would have helped if I could have, but I didn't want to.

- I can't help everyone, so it would be unfair to help this person.
- I didn't know how to help.
- People like that frighten me.

What reasons do we have for walking past people in need? Are they good reasons? If we can't stop for everyone, what else can we do?

Who deserves help?

Obviously some people become homeless when it's not their fault. For others it's tempting to say that their situation is because of their own foolish or wrong actions. When resources are limited, who should we help? Which of the following sayings of Jesus are most relevant here?

Do not judge, or you too will be judged (Matthew 7:1).

It is not the healthy who need a doctor, but the sick (Matthew 9:12).

Go now and leave your life of sin (John 8:11).

Why be hospitable?

As well as general instructions to live justly and to put into practice the good news to the poor, the early church was told to be hospitable. (See Hebrews 13:2 or Matthew 25:35, for example.) Why was hospitality seen as important in those days? Is it equally relevant today?

Ideas for action

There are many things you can do as a group or individually which can make a difference. Here are just a few in increasing order of difficulty:

- *Buy a copy of* The Big Issue. Smile as you do it; and read it.

- *Tell people where to get help.* Publicize Shelter's national housing advice helpline (0808 800 4444) on your church noticeboard.

- *Support the churches' voice on homelessness.* The Churches National Housing Coalition (CNHC) leads campaigns nationally and encourages local action. More members means more impact. Both individuals and churches can join.

- *Hold a Homelessness Sunday.* Held annually on the last Sunday in January, it provides a national focus on homelessness and bad housing. Two thousand churches do it so far, and the resource pack from CHAS (see end of chapter for details) is excellent.

- *Volunteer!* Most local projects depend on volunteer help and never have enough. You might make all the difference. Start at one session a month and work up. Enquire locally.

- *Put your money where your faith is.* Invest your church building fund (or your savings) in the Just Housing Account run by the Triodos ethical bank. You get interest on your savings and Triodos lends vital funds to housing projects. For example Caring For Life is partly financed by a Just Housing Account loan.

- *Help new tenants with a starter pack.* Moving into a new flat without even the basics to get started is highly demoralizing. Some groups have got together to give out starter packs of soap, cereal, sugar, a dishcloth, washing liquid, sponge, towels ... whatever. This is an excellent idea that builds friendships and makes a real difference.

- *Set up a rent-deposit scheme.* Many young people can afford to pay rent but don't have the deposit they need to get started. It's easy to set up a fund that guarantees their deposit and lets them move in. Many groups do this – there's even a national association – but more are needed.

- *Set up a Nightstop scheme or join an existing one.* (See end of chapter for details.)

Do's and don'ts

- Do smile.
- Do help one person at a time.
- Do remember that homeless people are just people who don't have homes.
- Do … something.
- Do see the person that God loves.
- Do start small.
- Don't give up.
- Don't do everything on your own.
- Don't be naïve about drugs.
- Don't judge.

Further help

There are many excellent resources. For up-to-date information the Internet is ideal.

Churches National Housing Coalition (CNHC)
Central Buildings
Oldham Street
Manchester M1 1JT
Tel: 0161 236 9321
E-mail: coalition@justhousing.co.uk

The resource pack for Homelessness Sunday is a comprehensive resource. (Also available on disk.) It costs £5 from:

Homelessness Sunday
c/o Catholic Housing Aid Society (CHAS)
209 Old Marylebone Road

London NW1 5QT
Tel: 020 7723 7273
E-mail: dan@chasnat.demon.co.uk

Two charities, CRASH and JRF, have combined everything that anyone knows about single homelessness into three books which they're giving away free to voluntary agencies. Call 020 8742 0717 or e-mail crash@clara.net

Visit www.centrepoint.org, Centrepoint's award-winning Website, to find out what it feels like to be homeless and whether you could cope.

Browse www.housing.detr.gov.uk/information/rough/, the Rough Sleepers Unit Website, to find out what the government is planning.

For authoritative research on everything to do with home-lessness and housing, visit www.jrf.org.uk/jrf.html, the amazing searchable library of the Joseph Rowntree Foundation.

Visit www.caringforlife.co.uk/caring/index.html, the Web-site of Caring For Life, another local project.

For information on a Just Housing Account loan, call free on 0500 008 720.

For a Starter Pack call the Scottish Churches Housing Agency on 0131 477 4556, or e-mail diane@scotchho.org.uk for more information.

For information on a Rent Deposit Scheme contact:

National Rent Deposit Forum
Suite 305
Lonsdale House
Blucher Street
Birmingham

Tel: 0121 616 5067

To set up a Nightstop scheme, write to:

Nightstop UK
45 Otley Road
Shipley

Children with a future

Keith White

In 1899 Herbert White, a young Sunday school teacher in east London came into contact with a little girl, Rosie, whose mother had just died. She was an only child and her father was an alcoholic. Distressed and without even a pair of shoes to wear she turned to him for help. She was afraid that she might end up in a workhouse. It was a poignant encounter for Herbert was himself motherless and his heart was overwhelmed with compassion for her. Put another way, he didn't have the normal defence mechanisms in place that would have allowed him to refer her elsewhere!

A fellow Sunday school teacher agreed to take Rosie into her flat above the shop where she worked, much to the relief of her father. Herbert White, who was a bank clerk, looked after the financial needs of the arrangement from his own earnings. And so began not only a rebuilding of Rosie's life and self-esteem, but also a remarkable story of childcare provision.

A hundred years later the initiative of Herbert had resulted in over a thousand children being cared for in the same neighbourhood. There is now a unique, thriving family home here with doors open to children and families in need. Herbert's son Victor continued the vision and I am the third generation of the same family, living in the same house. There is a pre-school nursery, a school for children with cerebral palsy on the premises, a mother-and-toddler group and lots of activities for children and families in the neighbourhood. The name of the residential community is Mill Grove.

The home does not seek publicity nor funding and is little known. The whole venture is a work of faith with the family daily trusting God to meet all its needs of shelter, food, clothing or finance. It is used by neighbours, local churches and local authorities.

In May 2000 there was a family reunion on a grand scale. Those who had lived at Mill Grove during their childhood returned with spouses, children and, in some cases, grand-children. And they came from all over the world, including the USA, South Africa, Holland and Australia. Perhaps the most precious discovery was the way in which many of those who had been cared for as children had been able to show consistent love and commitment as parents in their own families. Potential cycles of deprivation had been broken.

Rosie kept in touch with the family long after she had left and Mill Grove continues to be a family for life. Every child knows that he or she can always rely on the love, prayers and support of Mill Grove, and there is a lively informal family network worldwide. It is a Christian family with links with all the main denominations, and many of the youngsters have found faith in Jesus during or after their stay.

Issues for discussion

Explore what Jesus meant when he called a little child to stand in the middle of his disciples to demonstrate who is greatest in the kingdom of heaven. (See especially Matthew 18:1–14; Matthew 19:13–15; Matthew 21:12–16.)

There is an essential connection between childhood and the kingdom. Put simply, the church like every other social institution, is run by adults. It tends to have similar characteristics to other contemporary organizations. But God's kingdom is 'not of this world'; it is completely distinctive, and if we begin to understand and connect with children we are given special insights into God's heart and way of doing things. This seems to be the key element of what Jesus is trying to communicate.

- What are the ways in which we can marginalize children in ordinary church life, especially those who are 'unchurched'?
- How can we introduce more stories and images into communication by Christians that will be relevant to the children of today?

The basic needs of children

In caring for children for over twenty years and exploring childcare theory with my Bible open I have come to suggest five basic needs:

- *Security*. Every child longs for the experience of Eden (Genesis 2) in which there is a relationship or place that is completely secure. Usually this will be a biological family and a family home, but ultimate security goes deeper than this – all earthly security is temporary. Short-term projects and involvement with children can undermine their sense of security.

- *Significance*. This security is not about money, record-keeping or buildings. It is found through relationships with people who know a child by name, who are known by the child, and where both know they are uniquely special to the other. (See, for example, Hosea 2:21–23.) Such people are irreplaceable, so it follows they will not usually be professionals whose relationship is bound by time and contract. Bob Holman has used the term 'resourceful friends' to describe the role that is so important to children and young people who lack consistent parenting advocates.

- *Boundaries*. However much a child seeks to test and stretch them, he or she needs and thrives on firm and consistent boundaries. (See Matthew 5:17–20.) These include patterns of life, examples set by adults, as well as discipline. Moral and spiritual teaching is a vital element of the process.

- *Community*. Children long to be a part of groups, teams and clubs in addition to their own families. Peer groups at school and in the local community are particularly important. (See Acts 2:42–47 for a tight-knit community.) It is not enough simply to see children as individuals in isolation, or as family members. Most long to belong.

- *Creativity*. Children love to play, to mimic, to move, to sing, to dance, to make things. They are made in the image of their Creator (see Ephesians 2:10) and need an environment in which they can express themselves fully. That applies to the family home, school and neighbourhood. Without that space they become bored, depressed and frustrated. Repressed creativity can turn inwards, or outwards towards violence.

What other needs would you identify from your experience? How can some of these needs be addressed by your home group?

Jesus warned about child abuse
(see Matthew 18:7–9)

Sadly, we are increasingly finding Christian organizations and churches where children have been physically and emotionally abused in the past. There is also much concern about unborn children, and children who experience divorce and the separation of parents. And all the time there is the blight of poverty on whole classes and neighbourhoods of children and young people.

How could their anguish and pain have escaped our notice? Perhaps it is because children are not at the heart of our understanding of God's Kingdom that they have been allowed to suffer so chronically. We need to consider whether teachers, youth workers, Sunday school teachers and parents are valued as highly as the teaching of Jesus implies they should be.

How much do we know about children in our local community, and how can we find out more? What action has our church or group taken to ensure the adults responsible for children's activities are rigorously checked?

(A word of warning at this point. If you find you are out of your depth then ask a leader to contact the Churches Child Protection Advisory Service. They will be ready and willing to help you with the next steps to take.)

Ideas for action

- *Praying for and supporting parents and teachers.* Churches have many parents and teachers in membership. Every one is under some form of pressure or another as they seek to build a future for children, yet they rarely feel supported, understood and prayed for. We may need to take the pressure off them by easing expectations of what they might do on behalf of the church in order to affirm their primary roles with children.

- *Assisting the local school.* Perhaps one or more members of your group could offer to support the local school or schools in a voluntary capacity. This could range from school governorship through to attending school trips and reading with children. Help at dinner time can also be invaluable.

- *Support for local schools workers.* There is a growing number of Christian school and youth projects. If you don't know it, then try to find the name of those involved in your area. They would be delighted to have your prayer and practical support. They have wonderful opportunities to help youngsters through assemblies, teaching, clubs and friendship.

- *Foster care.* This is obviously a major commitment and it will be a realistic option for only one or two in your group at the most. But sharing our home and family is a highly practical way of helping children and young people. Your church or group might be able to support and encourage any who are already foster carers.

- *After-school activities.* The critical period for the physical well-being and protection of many children is that immediately after school and before a parent comes home from work. Perhaps your church could provide a safe space for play and homework one evening a week.

- *Pre-school facilities.* Many parent-and-toddler groups, pre-school nurseries, and government projects like Surestart are provided or spearheaded by churches. It might be worth finding out whether there are any gaps in your area, or groups that would welcome your help. Contact the local Preschool Playgroups Association or the Under-Fives Officer at the local council.

- *Safe play space.* One of the biggest changes affecting children's lives in the past generation has been the decline of safe play space, whether in urban or rural areas. A garden belonging to one of your members, or the area immediately around your church might be a godsend to children and families.

- *Christian organizations for children.* Crusaders, Boys' and Girls' Brigades and the like are all finding great difficulty recruiting leaders – yet they provide unique training and opportunities for children in the name of Jesus. It may be that one of your group could help out.

Do's and don'ts

There is no substitute for talking with parents, those responsible for teaching children, and the children themselves, to find out what the stresses and opportunities are in a local area. This process means the church listens to people and can develop priorities appropriate to the area. The list of ideas above is just a brief set of examples based on the needs of children. In reality there is no end to the modest and practical steps a Christian group can take to improve the well-being and life chances of children.

It is vital to encourage

- careful listening and planning in a clearly defined area;
- participation in existing organizations and activities;
- full-scale vetting of all adults put in a position of trust;
- the involvement of children and young people in any proposals;
- the full support of the whole church;
- lots of regular prayer.

It is vital to avoid

- letting your heart rule your head and becoming over-committed;
- allowing unsuitable and unchecked adults to be in direct contact with children;
- starting unsustainable projects which then let parents and children down;
- action which takes no account of local potential and needs;
- anything which puts more pressure on parents and teachers;
- activities which encroach on the life-space of other children and young people (some open youth clubs have spoiled existing groups because boundaries have not been considered carefully enough);
- overlapping and competing projects.

Summary

Children and young people are special gifts from God. Their ways are not our ways, their thoughts are not our thoughts and sometimes they will help us with glimpses into God's kingdom and his way of doing things. They have tended to be marginalized in corporate Christian life and worship and there is a crisis in many churches and denominations, where children's work has effectively ceased. A community approach will open up new ways of serving children in the name of Jesus, the One who insisted they were central to any understanding of God's purposes.

Further help

Care for the Family
PO Box 488
Cardiff CF1 1RE
Tel: 02920 811 733
E-mail: Care.for.the.Family@dial.pipex.com
Website: www.care-for-the-family.org.uk

Scripture Union
207 Queensway
Bletchley
Milton Keynes MK2 2EB
Tel: 01908 856 000

Catholic Child Welfare Council
St Joseph's
Watford Way
Hendon
London NW4 4TY
Tel: 020 8203 6323

The Children's Society
Edward Rudolf House
69 Margery Street
London WC1X 0JL
Tel: 020 7837 4299
Website: the-childrens-society.org.uk

Churches Child Protection Advisory Service (CCPAS)
PO Box 133
Swanley BR8 7UQ

Rebuild

Tel: 01322 667 207
E-mail: pcca-galro@msn.com

Christian Child Care Forum
Tel: 020 8504 2702

Churches Together for Families
27 Tavistock Square
London WC1H 9HH
Tel: 020 7387 8413

Spurgeon's Child Care
74 Wellingborough Road
Rushden NN10 9TY
Tel: 01933 412 412
E-mail: scc@spurgeons.org
Website: www.garrick.co.uk/spurgeon.html

15

Twenty-first century youth

Roy Crowne

There has long been a communication gap and a great deal of suspicion between the church and non-Christians (especially young non-Christians). This gap is growing ever wider and needs to be bridged. To do this we need to follow Jesus' example and meet people's needs in a way that is relevant to them. This can only be done if we understand and value their culture, beliefs and language.

Read through any Gospel and you will see that Jesus related to different people in different ways. He had no formula: he used different tactics each time he spoke to someone and, importantly, he met both their physical and spiritual needs. His was not a static set of ideas but a relationship! Rather than presenting them with a set of dry facts about his life, we need to help young people to have a dynamic relationship with Jesus.

The gospel is not just about preaching; it is also about demonstration. People should have the opportunity not only to hear the gospel but also to see, understand and experience it. Young people need to be given time to see God's love in action and then to try it out on the quiet and 'dip their toe in'. This is a more realistic way of looking at evangelism than the 'preach and response' method. Teenagers are not interested in empty words and arrogant claims to knowing the whole truth – they seek something that works and will look carefully at the people around them. To be effective evangelists we therefore need to form relationships and live the gospel as well as preach it.

Above all we need to go out into the community rather than sit in our churches expecting people to come to us. There is currently a great mistrust of institutions (including the church). An organization needs to be seen to be engaging with people's lives in positive ways before it will gain any respect.

What does the Bible say?

- Mission has its origins in God who, for our sake, became human and was unashamed to call us his brothers, sisters and friends. Consider Genesis 1; Philippians 2:5–11; Romans 5:8–9; Hebrews 2:11; and John 15:15. How does God reveal himself to be a God of mission? What implications might this have for our lives?

- Read Matthew 18:1–6; 1 Timothy 4:12; 1 John 2:12–14. What does this reveal about God's heart for the young? How does this turn our concept of young and old upside down?

- Look also at the following passages: 1 Corinthians 9:22b; Matthew 9:36–38; Matthew 28:19–20; and Proverbs 22:6. In Jesus' day gathering the harvest was a job that involved everyone, men, women and children, young and old. How does youth work fit into what we are instructed to do as followers of Christ?

- Youth work is also not only about what we, as the church, can give young people; it is also about what young people can bring to the church!

- Read Acts 2:17; 1 John 2:14; and 1 Timothy 4:12. What part should young people be playing in the church?

- It is also worth considering these heroes of the Bible:

Joseph (Genesis 37:2); Joshua (Numbers 11:28); Samuel (1 Samuel 12:2); David (1 Samuel 16:11); Josiah (2 Chronicles 24:1–3); and Mary, Jesus' mother (Luke 1:27).

Ideas for action

A simple yet important place to start is by encouraging youth workers already employed in your church or area. Full-time youth ministry is a taxing job and the knowledge that people are praying for your work provides reassurance. Melanie Stand, a youth and family worker at St Boniface Church, Quinton, Birmingham, says, 'You need a support structure behind you or you will either give up or try and struggle continually. Prayer backing is an essential part of any ministry.'

Prayer for more general things such as a local school, youth project or a gang is also a good start. However, while prayer is vital, we are also called to be people of action. As Andy Hickford says in his book *Essential Youth*, 'God wants to use us to answer our own prayers. Unless we are giving priority to quality time with non-Christians, how will they ever hear and see the gospel? To pray for revival without making every effort to form genuine friendships with non-Christians is pure escapism!' (Kingsway, 1998, page 106).

You can ease yourself into youth ministry by first of all looking for little ways to help within your church. As Melanie says, 'It's the little things that make the difference, such as adults helping out at a bring-and-buy sale organized by the kids, or baking biscuits and cakes to take on residentials.'

Actually, doing things for young people is a great way of putting God's love into action and making them feel valued. This can include helping with projects or homework, providing transport to different events, giving references for jobs, and so on. The possibilities are endless and the impact this kind of attention makes is amazing. As well as practical support, affirmation and encouragement are also extremely important in a teenager's life. Never underestimate the power of a compliment! Compliments passed from adults to young people are especially important.

Setting up or helping out at a regular church youth club is also a positive idea. Programmes like Youth for Christ's 'Rock Solid' (three years' worth of materials for 11- to 14-year-olds) deal with life skills and other issues and are therefore relevant to young people's lives.

Out into the community

When it comes to going out and building relationships with young people, each of us is different. It is a good idea to pray about what situation will suit us. Here are a few suggestions of how to make an impact on the youth in your area.

Holiday clubs or activity days are one way to start, especially at the end of the long summer break when money is running low but boredom is on the increase. This can be as easy or as complex as you like: competitions, sports, games, art or drama are all excellent things to try. The advantage to this approach is that it serves the community in a positive, visible way.

In his book *Youth Culture and the Gospel*, Pete Ward provides guidelines on how to go about meeting and forming relationships with young people on the streets (Marshall Pickering, 1992, pages 54 to 56). He suggests that you first of all pray, seeking God's will and asking him to give you strength. He then recommends researching your area and visiting the places where young people tend to congregate (shopping centres, parks, and so on). Spend time there, making mental notes about any young people you might see. Once this is done you should start to visit a couple of these places on a regular basis. After a while you should be able to decide which group of young people you feel the most comfortable with and the most confident about striking up conversation with.

While this may sound daunting, meeting non-Christian teenagers may involve something as simple as volunteering at your local secular youth club or on a soup-run, or even at your local school. Which brings us to the next point.

Spiritual development is one of the aims of secular youth work and education. This, as well as a common interest in subjects such as sex education, citizenship and politics, is often used by Christian organizations as a way into schools. Or you can become involved in outreach to youth in your community by enquiring about Christian school workers operating in your area. If you do go into a school it may be worth bearing in mind that creative arts, sports teams and other interactive methods of teaching can enhance your communication with young people.

Another possible contact with schools can be through mentoring schemes or something similar. There are many opportunities via this route. Bridget Shepherd is employed by Blackheath School in Greenwich as a pupil support worker. Her job involves talking to individuals and small groups about their week at school and at home and helping the pupils to address any problems that may arise from these chats. She says, 'Young people respond well to someone caring and taking an interest, for instance buying a card and a bar of chocolate on their birthday. They love to talk about themselves and the relationship that comes out of spending time with each other is staggering. It's similar to a parenting role or that of a big sister.'

Getting involved in this kind of scheme does not necessarily involve a career change, though! Many local councils now run similar schemes and advertise for adult volunteers to participate. You can make enquiries to your local education authority or the department in your borough that deals with children and young people. Alternatively, if you own a business you could contact the Local Education Business Partnership who organize work experience placements for young people. The Training and Enterprise Council is also a useful contact.

Do's and don'ts

- Do give young people the opportunity to get involved in social action. Seeing God working in and through them and taking risks and finding God there can be an

137

amazing source of growth.

- Do remember what young people tell you – including their names! Treat anything they say as important.
- Do work with young people rather than against them. If a group are causing trouble try to redirect their energy rather than putting a dampener on it.
- Do find out what other local churches and organizations are doing in the way of youth work and try to coordinate your efforts.
- Do ask about your church or school or youth club's good practice guidelines for youth work (for example 'Safe From Harm').
- Don't expect things to happen straight away. Relationships take time to develop.
- Don't preach at young people. Without forcing it, chat about Jesus in conversations and show how Jesus is relevant to the whole of their lives (this means no 'God slots'). Jesus often taught people in answer to a question, which was prompted by the way he lived his life.
- Don't base the time you give to a young person on their reaction to the gospel. True friendship is unconditional!
- Don't think you have to have all the answers – there's nothing wrong with referring young people to a pastor, counsellor, doctor or other expert help.
- Don't assume you know what young people want – ask them!
- Don't try to be something you are not. Teenagers want adult friends with an experience of life, not adults pretending to be just like their other mates.

Just one mum

Maggie watched her teenagers growing and with them grew a vision to invest in the lives of those who didn't go near any church. So she volunteered to help out at XLP, a schools project run across several London Boroughs in conjunction with the Ichthus Christian Fellowship. She has become an invaluable member of the team. Among other things Maggie has set up prayer groups to support Christian teachers in several schools, and for the XLP workers as they spend time with young people mentoring, sharing Jesus, and supporting them in their life issues. Although she is now heavily involved in the youth work of the church she doesn't profess to be an expert – but being a mum has had its uses!

Further help

Youth for Christ
Church Resource Department
PO Box 5254
Halesowen B63 3DG
Tel: 0121 550 8055
E-mail: YFC@compuserve.com

Crusaders
2 Romeland Hill
St Albans AL3 4ET
Tel: 01727 855 422
E-mail: email@crusaders.org.uk
Website: www.crusaders.org.uk

Church Pastoral Aid Society (CPAS)
Athena Drive
Tachbrook Park
Warwick CV34 6NG
Tel: 01926 458 458
E-mail: info@cpas.org.uk
Website: www.cpas.org.uk

Frontier Youth Trust
Fourth Floor
70 City Road
London EC1Y 2BJ
Tel: 270 7336 7744
Fax: 270 7324 9900
E-mail: frontier@fyt.org.uk

Rebuild

Website: www.fyt.org.uk

YMCA England
640 Forest Road
London E17 3DZ
Tel: 020 8520 5599
Website: www.ymca.org.uk

YWAM England National Office
Highfield Oval
Ambrose Lane
Harpenden AL5 4BX
Tel: 01582 463 300

Tackling addiction

David Partington

'Looking back I recognize God's hand on my life even in the darkest times. It was as if once I had committed myself to him as a teenager he would not make do with a second-best relationship with me. Despite my stubbornness and self-reliance he brought me to a place of submission where all I could do was abandon myself into his grace and love. From a young child my life had been controlled by a need to be liked and loved. I was convinced people would only love me if they could get something from me. I found myself always feeling I had to purchase love and affection through what I could do. To find the reality of Father God's unconditional love really released me and enabled me to start to become the person he knew I could be all along.'

Martin

When I first met Martin his life was a shambles. Alcohol had all but taken away any self-respect, and any hope in a future, without drinking himself constantly into a stupor, was almost lost. Incredibly, by the power of God and the love of Christians, all that changed and, over ten years later, he's living a radically different life.

Real-life answers

Martin was somewhat unusual in that he had an experience of God before he began his slide into addiction. He acknowledges however that Christianity became for him an intellectual, 'gritted teeth' experience as college, a good job and marriage followed. Eventually, he writes, 'The dryness of the church drove me away and our social life centred around the village pub and that was where I turned to unwind and cope with living.'

Stresses at work and at home led to his drinking almost continuously and, by 1987, he had lost his job and his wife sued him for divorce. He moved back home with his parents and, although things got easier for a while, guilt and insecurity from the past drove him into alcoholism. This meant not only further despair and heartache for Martin but it also impacted miserably on his parents – for years. Eventually they found the courage to love him enough to tell him that unless he got help he would have to leave home.

Martin came to the following conclusion: 'I realized that the problem was in me and not in my surroundings. At this point I heard of Yeldall Manor (a Christian rehabilitation centre) through contacts with High Street Baptist Church, Isleham.' He was accepted on the Yeldall programme and stayed there for seventeen months, during which he learned to trust God more than himself. In 1991 he moved back home and immediately got his present job. He has been wonderfully and consistently discipled at the High Street Baptist Church where he also met and married his new wife, Kathryn. In time he also initiated a regular 'Overcomers' group that helps other people with life-controlling problems to find the freedom God has for them.

What does the Bible say?

Listed below are a number of verses from the Bible. Work your way through them considering how they might be appropriate for anyone struggling with life-controlling problems. This is not so that we can give proof texts to people but is to remind us of the resources available from God:

- looking for an excuse to sin – 1 Corinthians 10:13
- feeling trapped – John 8:36
- fearful – 2 Timothy 1:7
- doubting God's love – Isaiah 53:5–6
- feeling we're too sinful – 1 Timothy 1:15
- thinking we're going to fail – 2 Thessalonians 3:3
- feeling weak – 2 Corinthians 12:9–10
- tempted – James 1:2–4.

As you have gone through these, and explored their application, members of the group will probably be aware of some personal application in their own lives as well. Therefore, give time to share any insights and pray for each other in pairs before looking at the rest of the chapter together.

People first

Martin's story goes a long way to communicating how God uses Christians and the local church to help people with addiction problems find real freedom. We can do it not only because we have resources others don't have, the resources of God's Spirit, but also because he loves them far more than we can ever do. It's also vital to remember, especially in the early stages of someone's journey to freedom, that it's not a *problem* we're dealing with but a *person* just like you and me. Although these are complex issues it's important we see them in the context of God's amazing resources of grace, love and power.

Another key lesson is that of underlining to people that God is not a God of 'No' but is a God who loves to say, 'Yes!' *Yes* to their need of genuine love and acceptance. *Yes* to their need for inner strength. *Yes* to the provision of a family and community. You and other members of your church, as you love them through the everyday actions of everyday life, will be one of the main keys to their grasping these truths for themselves.

Building bridges into the church

Everyone, and especially someone with life-controlling problems, is looking for love and acceptance. We begin by getting to know them, building relationships in their territory, not ours. As the relationship develops we can pray and seek out Christian and/or secular resources for help. But we mustn't rush – it took a long time for Martin to be ready for a rehabilitation centre.

Although we know that our church provides us with love and fellowship, for these people the thought of walking into a church can be a powerful turn-off. We can make it easier for them, however, and for ourselves! We can invite them to our homes for coffee and, when they feel comfortable, can ask them if one or two other people can join us next time. If the people we have invited are members of your midweek group, for instance, it's a short leap to asking the new-comers if they would like to meet with the whole group. Then, when it is appropriate to invite them to our Sunday service, they will walk into a place where they know lots of people.

The church's job

Remember that saving the addict is God's job! Jesus told us that our job is to make disciples, to help them know him more intimately. This takes time and commitment, especially from one person, chosen and trained by the church. I deliberately say, 'One person', because it's not only the addict who needs sustained and dedicated support; others in the church also need to know who has the final responsibility, whom to share issues with. Make sure that person is well-supported though. This not only ensures quality care but also helps to prevent misunderstanding or the manipulation of inexperienced people. People with an addiction are desperate to have their immediate needs met, and tend to manipulate others. This can be a long-established habit.

It may be that our church as a whole needs training to ensure that as many people as possible understand what the issues regarding addiction are. Such training will help to minimize the 'fear' factor of working with addicts, as well as clarifying the proper safeguards.

Building on the foundations

Another significant way of helping those with life-controlling problems in our church is by setting up a support group, like the one Martin began. Groups like Overcomers have developed a specific biblical approach to helping people with life-controlling problems find lasting freedom. They work well, not least because such groups are about people with problems helping other people with problems!

Some people may need a period of time in a residential setting, like Martin. If a person enters a rehabilitation programme it is essential to maintain our relationship with that person, even at a distance. When they have almost completed their programme, we should make plans not only to welcome them 'home' but to ensure they have the accommodation and family support they will need.

Working with people who have life-controlling problems is tough, but no matter how overwhelming the crisis with an individual appears, God will give us the wisdom we need – when we need it. The transformation that can take place in people's lives can be awesome, but we must remember that some will choose to walk away from the love that's offered. Some may even die! On the basis that God goes on loving us with extravagant love, however, we have no choice but to go on loving.

Families and addiction

Addiction doesn't happen overnight. People can slide into it over a long period of time, and in many instances may manage to hold down a job and hide things from their family for some time. The nature of any addiction, however, is that it controls a person and their ability to control it diminishes rapidly. That's when work colleagues and families start to notice that something is wrong and to be affected by the person's erratic behaviour. The stress for families can be enormous and, after possibly years of promises that 'this is the last time', disillusionment and despair can set in. Marriages may even break up, as in Martin's case.

If we have contact with families in this situation it is important to do a lot of listening. We should sensitively help them to face the truth and support them as they come to terms with it. A key question, and difficult to answer, is whether the person really *wants* to change. Whatever an individual's situation it is unrealistic to expect the problem to be resolved quickly.

Ideas for action

The following are some helpful basic principles for supporting families:

- We should remember that all family members will be affected by the problem.
- It is importance to establish a clear understanding about our involvement.
- We should encourage the family concerned to have clear boundaries for behaviour in the family that all have agreed on.
- We should encourage the family members to keep communicating with one another, and to acknowledge where mistakes have been made.
- We should encourage them to keep loving the addicted person, but not be doormats.
- We should find out what local professional support agencies and activities exist, if any.
- We should get advice from professionals, and help the

family to be in touch with them directly, rather than just through us.

* We should get support for ourselves as well, but must remember the importance of confidentiality. We must not share the situation widely in the church – even for prayer – as this can undermine those concerned, especially the family.

Further help

Books

Use and Misuse, Ollie Batchelor (IVP, 1999)
Kicking It, David Partington (IVP, 1991)
Alcohol and Other Drugs, George Ruston (Scripture Union, 1991)
Drugs: A Parents' Guide, Department of Health (HMSO, 1992)

Training in drug prevention

Hope UK
25(f) Copperfield Street
London SE1 0EN
Tel: 020 7928 0848 (24 hours)

Training in general addiction awareness

International Substance Abuse and Addiction Coalition (ISAAC)
21A Woodlands Avenue
Burghfield Common
Reading RG7 3HU
Tel: 01189 836 684
E-mail: isaacmail@aol.com

Life for the World Trust
Wakefield Building
Gomm Road
High Wycombe HP13 7DJ
Tel: 01494 462 008

Christian intervention/rehabilitation

Caleb House
21 Victoria Road
Clevedon BS21 7RU
Tel: 0127 534 1112

BETEL of Britain
Windmill House
Weatheroak Hill
Alvechurch
Birmingham B48 7EA
Tel: 01564 822 356

Yeldall Christian Centres
Yeldall Manor
Hare Hatch
Reading RG10 9XR
Tel: 0118 940 1093

Crisis Centre Ministries
12 City Road
St Pauls
Bristol BS2 8TP
Tel: 0117 942 3088
Website: www.crisis-centre.org.uk

Support groups

Overcomers
Townmills House
20A Bridge Street
Andover SP10 1BL
Tel: 0126 433 8999

Crisis Recovery UK
Earls Court Community Project
24 Collingham Road
London SW5 0LX
Tel: 0207 370 4424 / 0208 694 6125

E-mail: fgr.recovery@virginnet.co.uk

General enquiries

Evangelical Coalition on Drugs (ECOD)
Whitefield House
186 Kennington Park Road
London SE11 4BT
Tel: 020 7207 2100

DrugScope
Waterbridge House
Loman Street
London SE1 0EE
Tel: 020 7928 9500

Crisis Centre Ministries
12 City Road
St Pauls
Bristol BS2 8TP
Tel: 0117 942 3088
Website: www.crisis-centre.org.uk

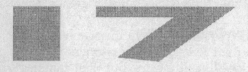

Prison: during and after

Peter Zimmerman

The 'Angel Tree' project

Susan, a prisoner's wife, nervously answered the door with her son Billy in her arms and her daughter Lucy clinging to her. 'It's all right, Billy, your dad hasn't forgotten you,' said Kath, the Prison Fellowship volunteer, as she held out presents.

Susan's first response was, 'They're not from my Ray. He's got no money for Christmas presents.' While his family were just about surviving in Kent, Ray, Billy's dad, was 300 miles away in a Yorkshire prison. When Kath explained she was from St Luke's, a local church, Susan warily invited her in.

The Christmas presents given through the Prison Fellowship Angel Tree project were just the start. Susan soon asked whether the church Sunday school would accept the children of a prisoner. Of course they would! Later, with Lucy and Billy attending regularly, Susan went along to a family service herself, and it wasn't long before she became a committed Christian.

Ray, who had heard about Angel Tree from his prison chaplain, soon had a letter from Susan with news of their new 'church family'. To her surprise, Ray's next letter told of his own attendance at chapel and that he too had committed his life to Christ.

Ray has served his sentence and is back in Kent with his family. Now the whole family worship together at St Luke's.

Kath wanted to help prisoners and their families. But why get involved in their lives? Aren't prisoners to blame for what they have done? Yes they are, but their families – including their children – should not have to suffer the consequences of their parents' crimes. The effects upon a prisoner's family can be devastating. Financial pressures, stigma, loneliness due to the loss of a partner, and often deep anger at being let down. Where the prisoner is a mother, who looks after the children? Sometimes family members or, where necessary, the children are taken into the care of the local authority.

The children of prisoners are possibly among the loneliest children in our country. In England and Wales

- there are over 120,000 children who have a parent in prison;
- two out of three prisoners have children;
- two out of three women prisoners are mothers of children under eighteen;
- four out of ten fathers in prison receive no visits from their children;
- prisoners' children are six times more likely than others to commit crimes.

Although the children are blameless, they too live in a kind of prison.

As each family situation is unique so too each prisoner is unique, and we must be careful not to stereotype individuals. Not all respond like Susan and Ray. Some prisoners will be remorseful and others won't; for some, prison will be a way of life, but for others it will be a frightening experience. Some prisoners may profess their innocence, and in a small number of cases they may well be innocent. We need to avoid being sentimental and naïve, however, but equally, we should not dismiss all prisoners as hardened villains. What is certain, though, is that prison can have a shattering effect upon both the prisoner and those closest to him or her, and there is a lot that Christians can do to offer constructive support both during and after a period of imprisonment.

What does the Bible say?

- In Matthew 25:31–46 Jesus describes to his disciples the Day of Judgment when he will come and judge all the nations. He mentions some practical acts of service, such as feeding the hungry, giving drink to the thirsty, welcoming the stranger, providing clothing and visiting those who are sick or in prison. These are illustrations and not meant to be exhaustive. It is clear from the constant repetition, however, that Jesus wants us to care practically for those in need, and not just those who are more deserving.

- Discuss how you feel about supporting prisoners, ex-prisoners and families who are often rejected by society? What are your fears and concerns? How can you overcome these?

- Read Matthew 18:1–5. This well-known passage makes it clear that welcoming a child in Jesus' name is like welcoming Jesus himself. Now read Psalm 10:17–18 and Isaiah 1:17. What do these passages tell you about God's concerns? How should these statements affect your attitude to the child of a prisoner? Consider the possible effects of not welcoming prisoners' children or even of turning them away. What might some of the practical issues be of getting involved with prisoners' children?

- Now read 2 Corinthians 5:18, 20. As Christians we believe that God has forgiven our sins through Christ's death and resurrection. We are therefore commanded to forgive others as God has forgiven us. We are also to go one step further and be involved in the ministry of reconciliation.

While many churches and Christians support and welcome prisoners, families and ex-prisoners, regrettably some do not. How do you feel about supporting and welcoming an ex-prisoner to your church? How might you be involved in the 'ministry of reconciliation', for example to those in the church who might want to turn away either the ex-prisoners or their families, or in situations where prisoners are estranged from their families?

Do's and dont's

- Treat people in prison or who are ex-offenders as individuals and not as a category of person.
- Remember that the person has particular weaknesses; therefore don't be unrealistic in your expectations.
- Try not to be shocked by their past life or personal revelations.
- Make sure to consult with professionals such as the prison chaplain, probation officers, or voluntary organizations like the Prison Fellowship, rather than trying to go it alone in your involvement.
- Remember that coming out of prison can involve a huge adjustment for both prisoner and family. The ex-prisoner will have some substantial hurdles to get over in order to re-enter the mainstream of life: money, accommodation, employment, relationships, stigma, and the pressure to take the easy way out and return to the previous lifestyle of crime.
- Beware of fostering unrealistic hopes.
- Encourage the development of independence and responsibility rather than trying to do for prisoners what they can do for themselves.
- Think through the boundaries of your involvement carefully.
- If your church is involved with ex-prisoners, protect the wider membership by having clearly defined final

responsibilities; and protect the ex-prisoner and his or her family by maintaining confidentiality about their circumstances.

- Get professional advice and set sensible boundaries if they are previous sex offenders (see the 'Further help' section in Chapter Fourteen).
- Check the facts if an ex-prisoner turns up at your church claiming to have become a Christian and wanting your help: phone the chaplain of the prison he or she has been released from.
- If an ex-prisoner has become a Christian, beware of premature exposure through the giving of testimonies, as that person will need time to consolidate in daily life his or her new-found faith.

Ideas for action

- A good place to start is by praying for your local prison; in many areas special prayer groups will already exist.
- Volunteering to visit prisoners in prison or prisoners' families: contact the prison chaplain, or the Prison Fellowship about their Angel Tree project or other forms of voluntary work.
- Get training for prison visiting.
- Your home group or church could offer to help the prison chaplain with taking services, providing musicians or worship leading, or involvement in small-group activities such as Alpha courses.
- If the prison provides a crèche for families visiting inmates, there will often be a need there for voluntary help.
- Writing to prisoners: the Prison Fellowship can provide guidelines for doing this.
- Supporting individual prisoners as they prepare for release, and also during their resettlement: build the relationship before they leave prison.
- Research beforehand what sort of practical steps they will have to take on leaving prison, such as finding

accommodation (details of Christian hostels can be obtained from the Stepping Stones Trust), registering with their probation officer, claiming Job Seekers Allowance and housing benefits.

- In preparation for Christmas, contact well in advance the prison chaplain or the Angel Tree project about ways in which you can provide support at what can be a desperately lonely time of year.

Bible study in prison

For the past twelve years, members of the Church of God of Prophecy in Battersea have been going into Wandsworth Prison on a weekly basis to help lead a Bible study group. Their visits are supervised by the chaplaincy department and are resourced by members of the Church of God of Prophecy's South-East Area Team of singers, worship leaders, preachers and teachers. Prison can provide plenty of opportunities for reflection, and church members have been able to come alongside prisoners, to get to know them as people and to offer informal support. Over the years a number of prisoners from the Bible study group have attended the church fellowship on release. This has given church members the opportunity to help ex-offenders get on with life again.

Further help

For ideas for action, resource material, training, prayer groups, and information about Angel Tree:

Prison Fellowship England and Wales
PO Box 945
Maldon CM9 4EW
Tel: 01621 843 232
Fax: 01621 843 303
E-mail: fi34@dial.pipex.com

Prison Fellowship Northern Ireland

39 University Street
Belfast BT7 1FY
Northern Ireland
Tel: 028 9024 3691
Fax: 028 9024 3691
E-mail: info@pfni.org

Prison Fellowship Scotland
110 Ellesmere Street
Glasgow G22 5QS
Tel: 0141 332 8870
Fax: 0141 332 8870
E-mail: pfscotland@cqm.co.uk

Alpha in Prisons
Holy Trinity Brompton
Brompton Road
London SW7 1JA
Tel: 020 7590 8250
E-mail: Prisons@htb.org.uk

The Stepping Stones Trust
PO Box 344
Richmond
Surrey TW9 1GQ

National Association for the Care and Resettlement of
Offenders
169 Clapham Road
London SW9 0PU
Tel: 020 7582 6500

What place the gospel? Social action and evangelism

Rob Warner

Jesus and social action

Christian social action finds its supreme motivation in the ministry of Jesus. His methodology provides a framework for our social action.

- *Jesus didn't just talk about God's love in theory; he demonstrated God's love in action.* In his healing ministry and in personal conversations, Jesus was concerned to meet people at their point of immediate need. In local-church social action we aspire to do the same.

- *Jesus' compassion was heartfelt.* There was no professional detachment in Jesus. The word used in the Gospels to describe his reaction to people in need means being torn apart in your guts. Other people's tragedies really got to Jesus, and he felt compelled to bring something of the love of God into broken and hurting lives.

- *Jesus sought the outcasts.* His ministry focused on the social, religious and medical rejects: the tax gatherers who were linked to Rome, the 'poor' whom the respectable religious considered beyond the pale, and those suffering from incurable diseases whom the healthy strenuously avoided. In short, if you were living at the margins of society, you were on Jesus' hit list of compassion. So who is on the margins in the area your church serves?

- *Jesus' compassion had no strings attached.* He didn't delay healing people until they had professed faith. Nor did he insist that if he healed someone they would have to become one of his followers. He took the risk of unconditional demonstrations of the love of God. He treated everyone as special, including those with notorious reputations, even though many showed no further interest in his message.

We can therefore sum up Jesus-style initiatives in local church *social action* like this. In the imitation of Christ, we seek to demonstrate God's love in action, in ways that are heartfelt, inclusive and have no strings attached. We love because we serve a God of love.

Jesus and evangelism

Christian evangelism similarly finds its supreme motivation in the ministry of Jesus, and so his methodology provides a framework for our evangelism.

- Jesus didn't just demonstrate God's love in action; he gave a verbal explanation of God's love. If Jesus' perfect expression of God's love was incomplete in his actions alone, even so our social action, however well done, is insufficient for a full proclamation of the Good News.
- Jesus' proclamation was inclusive. Jesus didn't wait in the synagogue for the religious to come to him. He went out among the people and declared that God's ruling presence and love are made freely available to all.
- Jesus' proclamation had clear strings attached. We can sum up his message as repent, believe, and live in the love of God. However, by no means everyone who heard Jesus decided to repent and believe. And his own crucifixion demonstrates that the way of love can be violently rejected. The message of grace offers us undeserved love, but we still have to decide whether to

make a response of repentance and faith. Jesus' offer of forgiveness and grace provides us with a conditional inclusivity.

- Jesus' proclamation provoked a mixed response. Jesus' proclamation was not only inclusive – proclaimed to all – but also divisive: some responded with living faith, others were intrigued, others indifferent and others downright hostile. Christians have sometimes defined evangelism as 'making converts'. But making converts is beyond us and such a definition of evangelism can result in our trying too hard and applying undue pressure. Manipulating people to force a superficial or emotional response may be gratifying to domineering personalities, but it has nothing to do with the authentic proclamation of the Good News of Jesus Christ. His call to faith was heartfelt, and even urgent, but he always respected people's autonomy, giving them space to make their own decision in response to his message.

We can therefore sum up Jesus-style *evangelism* like this. In imitation of Christ, we seek to proclaim God's saving love, seeking to communicate in persuasive but non-coercive ways to all kinds of people, presenting the need to repent and believe, in the hope and expectation that some will join us in living faith. We declare salvation because we follow the Saviour.

Tensions

It's clear that social action and evangelism are both grounded in the ministry of Jesus and the love of God. But harnessing them together in the local church is sometimes easier said than done. Both have their instinctive detractors: some distrust social action as a 'social gospel', fearing that the call to eternal salvation will be forgotten or neglected; others distrust evangelism, fearing that it will be pushy or needlessly offensive.

Those involved in social action often have a pastoral

motivation: they warm to the inclusive love of Jesus. Those involved in evangelism often have a sense of urgency: they want repentance and faith to be proclaimed without delay, even if some reject the message and turn away. As a result, the two groups of people may instinctively distrust one another. The social action team may fear that the evangelists could mess up all their patient work at building relationships with the unchurched and the marginalized. The evangelism team may suspect that the social activists are avoiding any direct declaration of the gospel, in order to pursue their aim of inclusivity. The groups can suspect one another of a lack of love: if the evangelists were more loving, they wouldn't be abrasive and divisive; if the social activists were more loving, they wouldn't deprive people of a clear presentation of the Good News of eternal salvation.

In practice, these fears and suspicions can lead to an uneasy truce. Those involved in social action don't want the evangelists to rock the boat. Their aims are long term and patient. Meanwhile the evangelists can feel excluded from the social action projects. Their concerns are short term and they look for results: definite conversion testimonies.

Both types of Christian can overstate their case. Some evangelists are tempted to say, 'Evangelism is all you need. Give up all these time-consuming community activities that don't deliver the spiritual goods. Let the local council get on with social action, while the church gets on with its rightful business – saving the lost.' But Jesus' works of love went far beyond the disciples and he clearly didn't restrict his mission to direct evangelism alone. The slogan 'Social action is no part of the gospel' is flatly contradicted by the ministry of Jesus.

Similarly, some social action specialists are inclined to say, 'Social action is evangelism. It's the best way of communicating the gospel in our world. Let's forget about direct proclamation and a call to conversion – such things are too often divisive and counter-productive.' But Jesus' perfect love included evangelistic proclamation, both to individuals and to crowds. The slogan 'Social action is evangelism' betrays common sense and the natural meaning of words. We don't commend cricket by saying it is football. We don't commend exercise by saying it is sleeping. We have no need to commend social action by trying to make it replace or redefine evangelism.

To say that social action is integral to the mission of the church is entirely justified by the ministry of Jesus. Mission in this broad sense of the totality of Jesus' words and works comprises social action and evangelism working in partnership together. When we set them against one another, as rival priorities, we betray the wholeness found in the ministry of Jesus. Holistic mission needs to be pursued in every local church where we seek to express the Master's priorities.

Practical difficulties

Paddy, Elizabeth and Jean had long since sent their own children off to school. But they had a vision and passion to serve those who look after pre-school children. Their mothers-and-toddlers group soon had to be renamed when *au pairs* and nannies started to come, and were found to be some of the loneliest people in that part of London. Then a few brave dads started to come: some were unemployed, others were taking a break from work while the children were young, and some were working flexible hours from home. All these groups were included in a 'Carers and Toddlers Group', which soon packed out the building every week. The organizing team wanted to make constructive connections between their church and the Group. But it was a struggle. There seemed such a gap between Wednesday morning and Sunday morning, and few were prepared to cross the border in either direction.

Even before we respond to the timely encouragement of the REBUILD initiative, churches already meet a huge proportion of community needs in the UK, perhaps most often through playgroups, carer-and-toddler groups, and provision for older people. It is therefore important to reflect on how well we are achieving healthy and constructive connections between evangelism and social action.

Two common problems stand out. First, in our desire to serve the local community, we can sometimes produce over-secularized activities; very caring, very inclusive, but no place for Jesus. I remember discovering at one church that their playgroup was extremely well run, but there was no indication whatever to the users that it was provided, and indeed subsidized, by the church. It might as well have been a secular playgroup doing no more than hiring church premises. Just as a Church of England school does not apologize for its Christian ethos, when we provide a church-based playgroup or nursery we need to find the confidence and creativity to give appropriate expression to our Christian convictions.

Second, because there is now such a huge cultural gap between the churched and the unchurched, it can sometimes prove difficult to persuade Christians to get involved as 'users'. In a carer-and-toddler group, some Christians are more comfortable being providers or group organizers than attending on the same terms as everyone else. They may quickly ask for a separate, specifically Christian group, where they feel more immediately at home. The same can be true for elderly Christians, who prefer to run a lunch club than to attend and eat the meal.

We need to encourage Christians to get involved and to relax in the company of the unchurched. For some, this is natural and their everyday environment. For others, it is difficult because they have become so accustomed to the separated lifestyle of the church subculture. To be useful, salt has to leave the salt shaker, and leaven needs to be in the dough to have an effect.

Uncomfortable questions to ask

- Is there a tendency to neglect either social action or evangelism (or both) in your church? Why do you think this is, and what can realistically be done about it?
- Take time to reflect on what the balance is in your own life. Are there particular reasons for this? And how would you like it to change, if at all?

- How can your church build better bridges between its social action and evangelism?

Life to the full

The local church to which I belong (kairos – church from scratch, www.kairos.org.uk) has begun to experiment with a life skills programme we call Life to the Full. We try to identify life issues that are equally relevant to Christians and the unchurched. The precondition of involvement for Christians is that we get real and stay real – no pretending that being a Christian means living a problem-free, stress-free, uncertainty-free, totally peaceful and triumphant life! We want to explore issues that cause concern in everyday life, and discover and demonstrate the relevance of biblical insights. Issues we address include surviving stress, learning to listen and encourage, managing money, marriage enrichment, parenting, handling conflict and difficult people, the pressures of work and coping with a famine of time.

So is this pastoral care and disciple-making? Yes, certainly. Social action? In its own way. Evangelism? Well, it's probably more accurate to describe it as pre-evangelism, making preliminary contact with people who are not yet ready for more direct and explicit presentations of the gospel. For us, this is a practical experiment in bridging the gap between social action and evangelism in the local church. We certainly don't have all the answers, but we are doing our best to ask the right questions.

Finally

There are no easy answers, and no local church can ever address every need among the people we seek to serve. We have to make difficult choices according to our vision and resources. But the wholeness we find in the ministry of Jesus clearly indicates that every church has a double calling and responsibility, seeking to express the Good News of Christ in both social action and evangelism.

The last word

Joel Edwards

As the twenty-first century approached there was a rush of creative ideas, all dedicated to leave landmarks to its arrival. From the controversial Dome to the numerous modest local initiatives, Christians and non-Christians all wanted to be linked to something which would remind them of the significant time-line crossed together.

A number of Christian leaders and agencies, however, wanted to mark the new era not just with a lasting tribute to the millennium, but with a vital contribution to our community. That's why REBUILD was launched. REBUILD is a Christian response to the millennium concerned not so much with buildings and landmarks as with a passion to equip and enable Christians to be good news in God's world.

Those of us involved with the Christian church for the past three decades will remember the times when church was largely a Sunday affair with little concern for the needs of the community around it. Thankfully, that has changed significantly. As I travel across the United Kingdom and other parts of the world, even the most pulpit-bound church leaders have discovered a passion to serve our community.

And so they should. For there is more than enough evidence in the Bible that caring for our community is an integral part of the Good News we talk about on Sundays. It's important to remember that Jesus not only spoke, but also went about doing good (Acts 1:1; 10:38), and the history of the church gives us many good models to work from. As Francis of Assisi once said, 'By all means preach the gospel; and sometimes use words.'

I have discovered that even where churches have a mind to do something useful, they are not always sure how to go about it. REBUILD exists to swap good stories, sharing ideas for action, encouraging and empowering local congregations to be good news down their street. It puts Christians in touch with those organizations whose expertise can help to develop responses to particular types of local need. And through REBUILD Community Weeks churches can try simple ways of 'tasting' community involvement.

In the twenty-first century poverty, crime, family breakdown and general despair are likely to remain with us. At the same time, there is a lot of talk about the relevance of the church in today's society. How do we bring together the question of the church's relevance and the needs of our communities? This cannot be done on the inside of our buildings alone. Our witness and value to society will be felt best beyond the walls, out in the community where real people have real needs waiting to be met. For the church is always at it's best as it becomes less concerned about itself and focuses on the needs of its community.

Like the Good Samaritan, we must go where the suffering is. And this is done most effectively as our small groups turn their energies outward to face the world, meeting people in the communities through prayerful action. If you take this book seriously, and put what it says into action, in these opening stages of the new millennium you will be seizing an opportunity to leave monuments of love and care to let our communities know that God is really for them.

Members of REBUILD, a coalition of over sixty Christian organizations and church denominations, are the authors of this book. We have come together with a common vision, that of encouraging and enabling local churches to get involved with the needs in their communities. We believe that God is passionate about people, and wants to see local communities become places of hope, belonging, and strong relationships. Our prayer is that this book will go some way towards encouraging its readers to take hold of that vision for themselves ...

Contributors are listed below in alphabetical order.

Fran Beckett
Chair of REBUILD, the national coalition of organizations responsible for writing this book. Chief Executive of the Shaftesbury Society, a national Christian social action charity working in urban regeneration and church-based community work, and providing 'whole life services' to people with disabilities. Speaker, author, and adviser to a number of organizations.

Brendan Bowles
The National Director of the Churches National Housing Coalition, an umbrella body committed to encouraging and equipping Christians to tackle homelessness and associated issues through practical action and campaigning. Author of a number of homelessness resource materials.

Julia Burton-Jones
National Coordinator of the Carers Christian Fellowship which was registered as a UK-wide charity in 1997 to give support from a Christian perspective to people caring for relatives and friends. Author and speaker.

Steve Chalke
Steve founded the Oasis Trust and various related initiatives engaged in social action and evangelism in the UK and internationally. Speaker, author and TV presenter.

Sharon Craddock
Christian Resource Coordinator for Trinity Care, a Christian-based company dedicated to providing whole-person care for older people and encompassing physical, spiritual, social and emotional needs.

Roy Crowne
National Director of the UK Youth for Christ organization which is committed to radical youth evangelism including schools work, resourcing local churches, and whole-person ministry in the community. Evangelist and speaker.

Paul Dicken
Founder and National Director of Through The Roof, recently merged with the Disabled Christians Fellowship, an organization providing resources, advice on accessibility and support for disabled people and their families. Author of a number of resource materials, and a speaker.

Joel Edwards
General Director of the UK Evangelical Alliance, and a bishop in the New Testament Church of God, Joel has a strong commitment to Christians being salt and light in society. The Evangelical Alliance exists to promote evangelical unity and to be a voice to wider society. Author, speaker, and former probation officer.

Jill Garner
Church Development Director with the Shaftesbury Society, the national Christian social action charity. The Church Development Department enables local churches to engage in meeting social need in their communities through provision of a range of resources, programmes and advice. A member of the REBUILD Executive.

Andy Hawthorne
Founder of the World Wide Message Tribe Christian rock band and of Message to Schools Trust. Andy is an evangelist who is convinced of the need to engage with the whole person and communities. Founded the EDEN Project in Manchester, and the Message 2000 youth initiative.

Nina Kelly and Eileen Jones
Nina is a freelance journalist and Publicity Officer for Positive Parenting; Eileen is the founder and Chief Executive of Positive Parenting, a national Christian organization promoting through resources, training material, and running courses on the importance of parenting skills.

David Partington
Was for twenty years Director of Yeldall Christian Drug Rehabilitation Centre, and is now General Secretary of ISAAC an international networking agency encouraging Christian action on addiction. Author and speaker.

Simon Pellew and Sarah Thomas
Simon is the Managing Director of Pecan, a Christian charity working with unemployed people in South-East London. Sarah is a literacy tutor with Pecan.

Mannie Stewart
Is the head of Social Responsibility for the UK Evangelical Alliance and is responsible for a number of strategic social action networks. He is the founder of Nottingham Christian Action Network (CAN) which became a model for over thirty CANs now operating across the UK. CANs map local Christian action and provide a forum for encouragement and development. Mannie is also on the Executive of REBUILD.

Keith Tondeur
Founder and Director of Credit Action, an organization set up to assist people with money worries through the provision of advice, training of debt counsellors, and a

range of resource material and awareness raising and preventative initiatives. Speaker and author.

Rob Warner
Rob is committed to pioneering radical ways of reaching unchurched people in a post-Christian culture. A trustee and member of the REBUILD Executive. Baptist minister, church planter, speaker and author.

Keith White
Is an associate lecturer at Spurgeons College, and Trustee of the Christian Child Care Forum and the Frontier Youth Trust. Chair of the Editorial Board of Children UK, and editor of the National Council of Voluntary Child Care Organizations' annual journal. Author of several books; lectures and speaks widely.

Peter Zimmerman
Office Manager for the Prison Fellowship (England and Wales), a volunteer-based charity which seeks through prayer and practical care to help, support and develop Christian ministry to prisoners, ex-prisoners and their families.

Thanks are also due to Tearfund for supplying stories from their overseas partners, and to those other churches and local organizations who have shared the stories of their own experience of working to rebuild individual lives and communities.